WHERE TWO TRADITIONS MEET

Thomas J. Morrissey SJ

Where Two Traditions Meet:
John Sullivan SJ
1861-1933

the columba press

First published in 2009 by
ᴛʜe coʟᴜᴍʙᴀ ᴘʀess
55A Spruce Avenue, Stillorgan Industrial Park,
Blackrock, Co Dublin

Cover by Bill Bolger
Origination by The Columba Press
Printed in Ireland by ColourBooks Ltd, Dublin

ISBN 978 1 85607 644 9

Table of Contents

Foreword

The Right Reverend Walton N. F. Empey

As I reflected on the writing of this Foreword, I found myself thinking, not of one but of two men who followed similar paths but whose lives came to very different conclusions.

John Tyrell was born in the same year as John Sullivan, the subject of this book, and both were Anglicans. Both of them converted to Roman Catholicism and subsequently were ordained as Jesuits. Tyrell eventually was removed from the order, suffered minor excommunication and was buried in an Anglican graveyard.

How very different was the life of John Sullivan who was to become a shining light of faith among his contemporaries. A stark contrast indeed.

The reader will be grateful to Father Tom Morrissey for giving a detailed account of the social and historic background of his subject. John was the son of Edward Sullivan who, as Lord Chancellor, was for a time the most powerful man in the land. As was the custom of the time, the girls of a family followed the faith of the mother and the sons that of the father. As Edward's wife was Roman Catholic so was John's sister. This custom was to change dramatically, and grievously for the Church of Ireland, with the promulgation of the *Ne Temere* Decree in 1907. However, it would seem that the household in which the young John was brought up was an extremely hospitable and tolerant one with few signs of sectarianism. Both parents had a deep influence on John's life. His father, whom he loved dearly, bequeathed to him his love of scholarship, while his mother gave to him a rich spirituality. Certainly two traditions were to meet in that respect.

As an old Portoran myself, I was pleased to learn that the school had a considerable influence on his life, not only through the Christian witness of its clerical Headmaster, Dr William Steele, but also of another former student whom he described as 'the most Christlike man he had ever met'.

How different his experience was to be when he entered Trinity College. Here, through well-known scholars Mahaffey and Tyrell, he was exposed to virulent sectarianism. It seems he was a reasonably good student but in lifestyle much the same as his contemporaries, leading a social life and fastidious about his dress. It was at this time of his life that he gave up church-going altogether until introduced to Mass, not by his beloved mother but by a skip or servant in the College.

Another influence which seemed to have stirred him deeply was his visit to the Orthodox monks of Mount Athos, some of whom were to keep in contact long after his visit. That visit led him to consider the possibility of discovering something more Western in ethos, which of course he was to find eventually in the Jesuits.

There is nothing to suggest that, unlike Tyrell, John was ever a devout Anglican, but following his conversion he embraced Roman Catholicism with great enthusiasm. That is where he found his true spiritual home. The change in his life was quite remarkable. The once young socialite enjoying good clothes and a good income through the practice of law, now becomes a school teacher living a life of extreme abstemiousness and simplicity. He had a high regard for the profession though it was generally accepted that he was not a very good teacher. Yet, as many testify, his whole demeanour and saintly manner of life had a profound effect on many of the students, who looked back on him with deep affection. The one brought up in the atmosphere of English power in Ireland now becomes the one who influences others to become Irish leaders in an Irish State.

We are grateful to Father Tom Morrissey for introducing us to this remarkable man.

Preface

John Sullivan's unusual life-story has given rise to two full-scale biographies, a number of pamphlets, a short documentary film, *Of Whom the World Knows Least* (1964), and has provided the inspiration for Ethel Mannin's successful novel *Late Have I Loved Thee* (1948). The biographies and pamphlets have been mainly about his remarkable life of prayer, penance, and healing. Relatively little has been said about the man's personality and life prior to his becoming a Catholic. This absence of information arises from the fact that he left scarcely anything in writing and was reluctant to talk about his earlier life. The purpose of this short book is to try to present something of the man, John Sullivan, in the context of his family and his times, availing of such clues as can be gleaned from the archives in Clongowes Wood College and from the previous books by Fergal McGrath and Mathias Bodkin.

The greater part of available material was presented in McGrath's extensive *Father John Sullivan, SJ* (1941) and in his later pamphlet, *More Memories of Father John Sullivan* (1976). Bodkin's *The Port of Tears* (1953) was a much shorter book, but had some fresh material and endeavoured to evoke the atmosphere of Victorian Ireland.

John Sullivan was in his mid-thirties when he became a Catholic. He was born into a position of privilege in an Ireland largely controlled by a Protestant minority. The second part of his career was spent among the Catholic majority. His life story built a small bridge, posthumously, between the two great religious traditions in Ireland, that of Catholicism and the Anglican tradition of the Church of Ireland. He enjoyed the freedom of Europe in the final decades of the nineteenth century, undertaking walking tours and making friends in France, Germany, Austria, Switzerland, Greece, and parts of the Ottoman Empire. He also moved comfortably in British society, practised law there, and like others of his class breathed easily the air of the British Empire. Yet, in the second part of his life, many of his students in Clongowes Wood College, Co Kildare, became prominent figures in a new Ireland, and seventy-five years after his death some of his maxims for life were quoted in Dáil Éireann by a Taoiseach of the Irish Republic. Truly, it would seem, a man with a message for different traditions, and for different religious, even political, persuasions; and one whose abandonment of opulence for a simple lifestyle challenges the compulsion to measure life in terms of more and more material possessions.

Introduction

John Sullivan's life, 1861-1933, had two distinct, almost equal parts. In the first, he was a favoured member of the privileged Protestant ascendancy. His father, as Lord Chancellor, was one of the most powerful men in Ireland, and John was known as a barrister, a classics scholar, and as possibly the most expensively dressed man in Dublin. In the second part of his life, he devoted himself to instructing schoolboys and to devoting every spare moment to prayer and the service of the sick poor. During this time, his patched and threadbare attire signalled his lack of interest in material possessions and public appearance.

At this point, a brief *resumé* of the political and educational background to John's life will be helpful. From 1800 to 1921 Ireland was part of the United Kingdom of Great Britain and Ireland. It was ruled by a British government and parliament. The parliament for most of that time was dominated by two great political parties, the Conservatives (or Unionists) and the Liberals. British rule in Ireland was represented by a Viceroy (or Lord Lieutenant), a Chief Secretary, and a Lord Chancellor, who was mainly concerned with the administration of the law. The leaders of the police, the army, and business were of the ruling class, usually members of the Church of Ireland, the established, recognised religion, to the upkeep of which all, Catholics as well as Protestants, had to pay tithes.

The Catholic majority, under a young barrister named Daniel O'Connell, formed in the 1820s a mass movement for civil and religious rights, which resulted in the Catholic Emancipation Act of 1829. This enabled Catholics to enter parliament, and to hold civil and military offices. O'Connell formed an Irish Party in the House of Commons and started a movement for the restoration of an independent Irish parliament. This was the beginning of what was called the Home Rule Movement. When this failed, a minority sought a solution by violence. The most striking example of this were the Fenians, members of a secret, oath-bound society, the Irish Republican Brotherhood, which sought, in the years of John Sullivan's early boyhood, to wage a violent campaign for Irish political freedom on three fronts: by dynamite operations in English cities, by the invasion of Canada, a British colony, from the United States of America, and by a successful revolution in Ireland. This last failed in 1867 and the movement went underground. It was succeeded by a revived Irish Parliamentary Party, which sought Home Rule under first, Isaac Butt, then Charles Stewart Parnell, and finally John Redmond. A Home Rule Act was passed in 1914, but because of its limitations it was rejected by many nationalists. Some of these brought about the 1916 Insurrection. This, in turn, led to a guerrilla war, which ended with the establishment of an Irish Free State in 26 counties of Ireland. Six counties in the north-east of the country remained part of the United Kingdom. John Sullivan lived to see something that he could not have envisaged as a young man, the greater part of Ireland under an Irish, largely Catholic, government.

It remains to say something about education. Where the majority population was concerned, there were very few secondary schools catering for their needs during the first half of the nineteenth century. Even at primary level, opportunities were very limited until after the 1830s. In the decade after the Famine, the Catholic bishops helped bring about a revolution at secondary level by encouraging foreign religious congregations and native congregations to set up schools. Around the same time, they established a Catholic University under John Henry Newman (later Cardinal). This failed because of lack of funds and because its degrees were not recognised by the government. This meant that there was no opportunity for Catholics to obtain university degrees. The bishops forbade Catholics, except in very exceptional circumstances, to attend Trinity College, the sole college of the University of Dublin, and the Queen's University, with its colleges in Belfast, Cork, and Galway.

Trinity College was founded in 1591, and from the start was associated with anglicisation and the promotion of the Church of Ireland. It produced many celebrated personalities and scholars. In John Sullivan's time, there were a number of outstanding scholars in the college, but there were also prominent professors who were openly anti-Catholic. This confirmed the Catholic bishops in their view that the faith of Catholic students was likely to be undermined in Trinity. The Queen's University was excluded by the hierarchy because no religion or theology was to be taught in its colleges, and their atmosphere was deemed to be secularist. In the circumstances, the bishops became leaders in a campaign for a university acceptable to the majority population. The government responded with the Royal University Act in 1879. This established a purely examining body, known as the Royal University of Ireland, which made it possible for the students of Catholic colleges to compete for degrees. The makeshift solution did not dampen the campaign for a Catholic University. The hierarchy invited the Jesuits to take over the old Catholic University buildings and to run a university college there. The director of University College Dublin, on St Stephen's Green, Dr William Delany, was determined to achieve such academic success in the Royal University examinations as to make an unanswerable case for the Catholics' right to a university. This meant achieving, with his unendowed college, better results than those of the heavily endowed Queen's Colleges. Within a few years, UCD on the Green outdistanced the combined results of the colleges of Belfast, Cork and Galway – a circumstance not lost on the professors at Trinity College during John Sullivan's time there.

The foregoing, hopefully, provides the necessary background to areas of the narrative that might be unfamiliar to many readers, and helps to situate John Sullivan in his place and times.

CHAPTER ONE

Family Background

John's father, Edward Sullivan, came from Co Cork. O'Sullivan was a long established family name in Cork and Kerry. Its association was Gaelic and Catholic. Some bearers of the name, however, dropped the O and became Sullivan and Protestant. One such was Edward's grandfather, James, who rose from a minor position to one of trust in the employment of the Jephson Norreys family, owners of Mallow Castle. In 1782 he married a Protestant, Mary Fitzgerald, and brought up his ten children as Protestants. All of them did well. One of them, Edward, chose to follow a business career in Mallow. He amassed a considerable fortune and purchased property in Co Cork before coming to Dublin to live. He was the father of Edward Sullivan the Lord Chancellor, and the grandfather of John Sullivan. He came to Dublin in 1861, the year John was born.

John's great-grandfather, mentioned above, died in January 1814. His funeral reflected the tensions over religious belief that were a feature of the nineteenth century in Britain and Ireland. He was reconciled to the Catholic Church before his death by the parish priest, Thomas Barry. But the family either did not know or determined, regardless, that there should be a Protestant funeral. The funeral service commenced in the Church of Ireland church but, as the parochial register for 19 January 1814 noted, 'James Sullivan was buried in part. Priests interfered and finished the service'! Although official records were destroyed in the Four Courts fire in 1922, the index to them survived and contains the *précis*:

> Funeral, complaints of priests' conduct at, corpse carried away by a mob at Mallow, Mass said, and harangue delivered at Cove churchyard.[1]

The formidable parish priest, supported by townsmen, carried away the coffin and gave it a Catholic burial. The members of the Sullivan family, however, remained staunchly Protestant.

Edward Sullivan

James's son, Edward, had four children: Edward born in 1822, James in 1824, Anne in 1826, and William in 1828. The last named became Clerk of the Records in the High Court, Dublin. His oldest brother, Edward (John's father), was educated at the Endowed School, Midleton. He entered Trinity College Dublin in 1839, and four years later gained a classical scholarship. He graduated in 1845. That year he was auditor and won the gold medal of the College Historical Society. In 1848, he was called to the Irish Bar, and ten years later became a Queen's Council. He rose to the top of his profession at a time of outstanding talent among Irish barristers. In 1860 he was named Third Serjeant, in 1861 Bencher of the King's Inns and Second Serjeant, in 1865 Solicitor-General, in 1868 Attorney-General, and later in the same year Master of the Rolls, which position he retained until his elevation to Lord Chancellor in 1883. In 1881 he received a baronetcy.

The *Dictionary of National Biography* drew attention to Edward's well-stored mind, his readiness, tenacity and eloquence. A Liberal in politics, he was returned to parliament for his native Mallow in 1865 and 1868, when his appointments as Solicitor General and Attorney General obliged him to seek a seat. As will be seen, he took a prominent part in many of the leading political and legal issues of the day. A lawyer of a slightly later generation, Judge M. M'Donnell Bodkin, KC, commented:

> It was said that the late Lord Chancellor Sullivan was for many years the real governor of Ireland, so faithfully did a succession of Lord-Lieutenants and Chief Secretaries follow his advice.[2]

Marriage and Family

Edward, as a young lawyer, settled in Eccles Street, Dublin. In 1850, he married Elizabeth Josephine Baily, daughter of Robert Baily, a wealthy land agent and property owner in Passage West, Co Cork. The Bailys were Catholics. They had five children: Annie, Edward, Robert, William, and John. As often occurred in the case of mixed marriages before the papal *Ne Temere* decree of 1907, it had been agreed that, in the event of there being a family, the boys would be brought up in the religion of their father and the girls in that of their mother. Elizabeth Sullivan, a devout Catholic, found it difficult that only one of her children was Catholic but she adhered firmly to her agreement.

Annie inherited her mother's deeply religious character. She devoted much time to charitable work, conducted a registry office for domestic servants, and as a member of the ladies' sodality at the Sacred Heart Convent, Leeson Street, from 1886, started the first scheme in Dublin for providing poor children with fresh-air holidays. The eldest boy, Edward, was called to the Irish and English bars, but devoted himself to literature and to the study and practice of book binding in which he became one of the authorities of the day. The second son, Robert, died young. William also studied law, was called to the Irish bar, and acted as resident magistrate in various parts of the country. William was born in 1860, just a year before John. He and Annie were greatly attached to their youngest brother. Although his mother was disappointed that her final child was not a girl,[3] John was warmly welcomed into the family and, as the youngest, was indulged.

CHAPTER TWO

John's Early Years

He was born on 8 May 1861 at No 41 Eccles Street, and was baptised on 15 July in St George's Church, George's Place, not far from Eccles Street. By the 1860s, however, the city's centre of gentility had shifted southwards across the River Liffey. In the year of John's birth, his ambitious father moved the family to Fitzwilliam Place, which had recently been built. As a result, John's nurse used to wheel the perambulator carrying him to the adjacent enclosed garden in Fitzwilliam Square, accompanied at times by Annie or a nine-year-old girl from the Dunne family who lived nearby.[4] He was remembered as a contented and smiling child, with blue eyes and golden hair. After a few years he had his own tutor, who helped to develop his proficiency in English and in the classical languages, but gave him no proper grounding in mathematics. All his life he felt incompetent in that area.

It is probably true that most people in western society are influenced for life by what is happening in the world around them in their early and adolescent years. In the Sullivan household, matters of political import were part of life. Edward's political friends called to the house, and this included the 'Grand Old Man' himself on more than one occasion. W. E. Gladstone is said, indeed, to have dandled young William and John on his knees. Few got that close to the great prime minister in a relaxed mood, when his eyes beamed and 'the very wrinkles about his eyes and mouth were expressive of good humour and delight'.[5] When John was four the American Civil War came to an end which, though much discussed in Ireland, would probably have meant little to him. Maybe he was brought, however, to the Dublin International Exhibition, which opened that May, 1865, at the Dublin Exhibition Palace and Winter Garden in Earlsfort Terrace.

The most discussed and feared phenomenon in Ireland and Britain in the 1860s was Fenianism. In 1866, when John was five, there were Fenian attempts to invade Canada, and the following year Fenian risings in Kerry, and subsequently around Dublin and other parts of Munster. In England there had been a Fenian raid on Chester Castle, the killing of a police sergeant in Manchester in an effort to rescue two Fenian prisoners, and an explosion near Clerkenwell jail in London that caused several deaths. What added to the relevance and excitement of it all was that John's father was standing for election in 1865 and 1867 and was known as a very strong opponent of Fenianism. Edward Sullivan was a small but dynamic lawyer and politician, who viewed Fenianism as the enemy of the entire system of law, power and patronage. He was determined to punish its proponents. He proved such a vigorous prosecutor of Fenians in Cork that he was jeered in the streets as 'Scorpion Sullivan'. His determined opposition was not something confined to members of the ruling Protestant ascendancy. Many middle class Catholics shared his views, including his close friend, Judge William O'Brien, who lived in nearby Merrion Square. The Catholic Archbishop of Dublin, Dr Cullen, moreover, denounced Fenianism, and sought a definitive condemnation from Rome.

One of the effects of Fenianism was to expedite government reforms, and to move the former Unionist, Isaac Butt, to take up the cause of Irish Home Rule. In November 1868 there was the excitement of a general election, which resulted in a victory for the Liberals, and the appointment of Gladstone as prime minister. On 1 March 1869, he introduced the bill for the disestablishment of the Established Church in Ireland. In preparation, Edward Sullivan, as Irish Attorney General, and Lord Spencer, as Irish Viceroy, visited him at his Hawarden estate in Flintshire, Wales. The following year, he met Edward and the Chief Secretary for Ireland, Samuel Fortescue, for three hours in London on the issue of Irish land reform.[6] John Morley, author and Liberal, attributed largely to Sullivan's guidance and influence the Land Act of 1870.[7]

In those exciting years, John must have picked up a great deal of what was going on from his brothers, if not directly from the conversation between adults. He was nine in 1870, which was also the year in which the eyes of Europe were focused on events involving France and Germany. In July 1870, France declared war on Prussia, and on 1 September suffered a devastating defeat, and the capture of its emperor, Napoleon III, at Sedan on the River Meuse, near the Belgian frontier. To add to the humiliation, the King of Prussia, William I, was proclaimed emperor of Germany in the Palace of Versailles on 18 January 1871. And in 1870 there had also been the siege of Rome by Italian troops, and the mixed reaction in Ireland to the event: the Catholics praying for the papacy and some actively participating in a papal brigade to defend the Vatican, while to many Protestants the Italian forces were viewed as representatives of democracy and progress against papal and clerical obscurantism. The situation in the Sullivan family must have been delicate, but since the family life appears to have been harmonious, it is likely that empathy for the feelings of Elizabeth Sullivan and Annie prevailed.

Although John Sullivan grew up among members of the Protestant ascendancy, his world and that of his family was not entirely closed where religion was concerned. The fact that Mrs Sullivan was a Catholic meant that her relations as well as Catholic friends of herself and her husband were welcome in the house. Indeed, a number of Jesuits appear to have been frequent visitors at some stage. These were said to have been the gifted Kelly brothers, Edward and Thomas, both accomplished classical scholars, and at a much later date, Fr James Cullen, founder of the Pioneer Total Abstinence Association. Judge William O'Brien, a fellow Cork man and friend from school days, went on holidays with Edward Sullivan, and dined with the family most Sundays. A further friend, a Limerick man, James Murphy, also a formidable prosecutor and married to a Catholic, had an estate, Glencairn, in Stillorgan, where Catholics and Protestants mingled freely, the Sullivan children were always welcome, and the celebrated wit and conversationalist, Father Healy of Little Bray, was a regular visitor.

John absorbed this relaxed, tolerant atmosphere. He learned to mix easily with senior men and women, and he became close to Judge William O'Brien and Judge James Murphy both of whom had a great affection for him. Most of all, though not yet consciously, he was influenced by his mother. In later years, he paid particular tribute to the influence of her deep faith and the example of her care for the poor. She went to Mass each day, a practice not entirely appreciated by her husband who complained to his friend O'Brien that he daily had his breakfast with only the servants for company.[8]

CHAPTER THREE

To Portora Royal School: an Abiding Experience

From this sheltered, friendly and caring background, John was extracted in 1873, when he was sent as a boarder to Portora Royal School, Enniskillen. He shed tears as he left home, but his parents had chosen well. The school, which had been established in 1608 by the royal charter of James I of England, to educate the youth of Fermanagh, and had moved from the streets of Enniskillen in 1770 to its present green site, had developed materially and academically under the able headmastership of Dr William Steele. Under his capable and kindly administration, new buildings were added, and high academic standards were achieved. John soon settled in. A younger son of Dr Steele remembered him as 'a very quiet, gentle-mannered boy and a favourite of my mother and her sister, Miss Haughton'.[9] He also, it seems, managed to be both studious and popular with the senior students.[10] Shortly before his death, John wrote of his time at the school, and paid a particular tribute to Dr Steele:

> He was a great Christian divine, an excellent administrator, just and fearless in his dealings, an admirable teacher of many subjects, but especially of the Greek and Latin languages.

> He also had a deep understanding of boys. 'Whenever he came among them, which was frequently, his approach was signalled by the vigorous shaking of a large bunch of keys.' In his fatherly role, he was almost always present at the boys' dinner, which he himself carved.

> On Sunday mornings, Dr Steele took the highest class in the library, where he elucidated for them the Epistle of the Sunday. John, to the end of his life, remembered vividly his headmaster's

exposition of the second chapter of St Paul's Epistle to the Philippians. With the Greek Testament before him, he commented on the remarkable Greek phrases used in the words which are translated in English: 'Let this mind be in you, which was also in Christ Jesus; who being in the form of God thought it not a thing to be clutched at but emptied Himself etc.'

Dr William Steele established good relations with Catholics in the area. On his appointment, in an expansive gesture that was also good business, he 'opened the classes of Portora to the sons of Catholic parents'. 'In my own class', John recalled, 'there were several Catholic day boys, and one of these was first in the class in Latin and Greek.'[11]

He remained six years at Portora, and won many prizes and medals. In the three years 1875-77 he was awarded the medal for classics. In the senior grade examinations of the Intermediate Education Board, in 1879, he came third in Greek, and had high, though not remarkable marks in Latin.[12] What he enjoyed most at Portora, however, was probably the relative freedom the boys experienced. He was not good at, nor interested in, team games, but he enjoyed rowing, and excursions in the school's several four-oared boats to one of the many wooded islands on Lough Erne. Sometimes they could remain out the whole day encamped on an island, where they made a fire and cooked meals. One island stood out in memory, the 'holy island' of Devenish. At the extreme end of the grounds of Portora College there was a place of departure for boats carrying the dead to their burial place on the 'holy island'. Portora took its name from the Gaelic original, meaning the 'Port of Tears'.

His own occasion for personal sadness occurred on 18 October 1877, when his brother, Robert, aged twenty-four, was drowned. The Sullivans had a villa called Undercliff at Killiney, Co Dublin. They were very friendly with members of another legal family, the Exhams, who had a residence nearby. On 18 October, Robert set out in a small sailing boat with two of the Exham family, John and Constance. They brought a gun for shooting at seagulls and Robert wore a heavy cartridge belt. A sudden squall capsized the boat. John Exham swam to an oar and clung to it. Robert seized the other oar and swam to Constance with it telling her to bear up, they would all be saved. Soon after, Robert sank, weighed down, it was thought, by the cartridge-belt. John Exham was rescued. His sister was found dead lying across the other oar. Robert Sullivan's body was never found, even though his family employed a diver to search for it.[13]

John Sullivan to his final years retained a sharp recollection of the anguish of those days, especially for his mother, when there was not even a body to grieve over. Her deep faith during that time made an indelible impression on him. On his return to Portora, he was met with deep sympathy and understanding from Dr and Mrs Steele. Not surprisingly, when he came to leave Portora in 1879 he did so with much emotion. He had secured a scholarship to Trinity College. It was to offer a very different experience to the blend of family, scholarship, and spirituality at Portora.

CHAPTER FOUR

Trinity College Dublin, and its impact

Of his time in Trinity College, John Sullivan, as a Jesuit novice, wrote modestly and briefly: 'I obtained a Royal School Exhibition at entrance (£30 a year; afterwards raised to £40) for four years. I failed to obtain a classical scholarship, though I tried twice. I took my degree in 1883, getting a senior moderatorship and a gold medal in classics. I had a taste for classics, but could do nothing in mathematics, and for that reason I had considerable difficulty in getting through some very ordinary examinations.'[14]

He studied under one of the most brilliant professors, R. Y. Tyrell, who was particularly noted for his mastery of grammar, idiom, and literary taste, but also for his dislike of drudgery, and of all the modern developments of archeology, epigraphy or the scientific study of manuscripts. According to a friend of John Sullivan at TCD, Henry Bowen from Kildorrery, near Fermoy, whenever Professor Tyrell came to a knotty point of history or archeology he appealed to John Sullivan, knowing that he had usually made up the matter in advance. The professor's reliance on his conscientious student became so marked, according to Bowen, that one day when John was unexpectedly absent, he refused to go on with the class.

Tyrell was a sparkling conversationalist, and a proven friend. Unlike his fellow professor, Dr Mahaffy, he stood by Oscar Wilde in his disgrace. Where Catholicism was concerned, however, he could be bitterly outspoken. Although, in Gladstone's words, Trinity College Dublin was 'perhaps the wealthiest college in Christendom',[15] the new assertive Catholicism in the post-famine years, more particularly the academic successes of University College Dublin under Jesuit management, and the strong nationalist criticism of Trinity's privileges as the sole college of

Dublin University, generated unease and anger among some professors in Trinity College, of whom Robert Yelverton Tyrell was probably the most vocal. In 1903 he printed in the *Students' Magazine* a scathing attack on the Catholic Church:

> ... a grim monument it stands
> Of cold observance, the incestuous mate
> Of superstition, destined of blind fate
> To draw the very marrow from the land's
> Poor starving delvers, and in empty air
> Scatter their wasted energies. Around
> It's huge ugliness scorns the common ground
> And point to Heaven; but to seeing eyes
> Each soaring steeple lifts its tall head and lies.

There was a storm of protest after the publication. Trinity College supporters had argued that Catholic students would suffer no disadvantage if they attended Dublin University, yet here was one of its most brilliant professors using the *Students' Magazine* to attack the church of its Catholic students. In a letter of explanation, Tyrell added to the furore and manifested the depth of his prejudice and anger. He had written the sonnet to protest against 'the undoubted fact that the Catholic clergy inculcate in their flocks cold acts of observance in lieu of sincere feelings of religion', and to denounce 'the ill-considered zeal of the rank-and-file of an unscrupulous priesthood, practising on the ignorance and superstition of an illiterate peasantry'.[16]

In his intemperate anger he played into the hands of very astute churchmen such as Archbishop Walsh and Dr William Delany, president of University College Dublin.[17]

It is not clear to what extent John Sullivan was influenced by this brilliant professor, who paid him much attention. There was also the other very brilliant and influential professor who made much of the son of Sir Edward Sullivan, himself a former distinguished student of the college. Dr J. P. Mahaffy was a man of great versatility, variously and conflictingly described as 'the last of the Olympians', 'an out-and-out snob', 'a singularly lovable and sympathetic person', an 'arrant humbug', 'an unclerical cleric' and many other names ranging from near idolatry to sheer venom.[18] By ordination a Christian clergyman, his focus was so much on Greece and Rome as to imply that Christianity had little additional to offer. In his case too, if less blatantly than Tyrell, there was a bitter anti-Catholicism. It appeared clearly in the case of his most brilliant student, Oscar Wilde, when the latter was feeling drawn towards Rome. 'No, Oscar, we cannot let you become a Catholic but we will make you a good pagan instead'; and on his way to Greece, he wrote boastfully to his wife on 2 April 1877, 'We have taken Oscar Wilde with us, who has come round under the influence of the moment from Popery to Paganism … The Jesuits had promised him a scholarship in Rome, but, thank God, I was able to cheat the Devil of his due'.[19]

There seems to be no evidence of Jesuits offering a scholarship or of being in touch with Oscar Wilde, but one of Wilde's Catholic friends, David Hunter Blair, had been encouraging him to come to Rome with him. Hunter Blair wrote in later years that when he subsequently met Wilde in Oxford he was 'changed'. He had become 'Hellenised, somewhat paganised perhaps, by the appeal of Greece to his sensitive nature, and Rome had retired into the background'.[20]

John Sullivan, in his turn, went on the Greek tour with Professor John Mahaffy. The only detail of the trip that has survived, however, is that when they visited the Acropolis, Mahaffy called on him to act as cicerone or guide to the party: a further recognition of the young man's preparatory work.

Greece made a huge impression on John Sullivan. He was to return there again and again, and he learned modern Greek as an aid to his travels. Did he too 'become Hellenised, somewhat paganised'?

On his own admission, he gave up church attendance during his time in Trinity. He later told how one of the 'skips' at the college (one of the servants), herself a Catholic, used to harangue the students about going to church on Sundays. One Sunday she assailed John on the subject. He replied that he was tired of going to church, since it meant nothing to him, but that if she would bring him to her church he would go. Startled, she agreed, and they went together. It is not known if the practice continued. It seems strange at first sight that instead of requesting to go with his mother or sister, or Catholic friends like Judge O'Brien, he opted to go with a servant. The reason may have been that he was curious about what went on at a Catholic religious service, but knew that it would prove embarrassing for his mother, Annie, and Judge O'Brien to be asked to bring him to a Catholic church because of the arrangement about the boys being Protestant, and, besides, his formidable father might not be pleased.

Doing Law

Edward Sullivan was reputed to be even more interested in Letters than in Law.[21] John showed similar tastes, demonstrating a keen interest in English literature as well as in the classical languages. On completing his Arts degree, nevertheless, he took up his father's other great interest, the study of law. In 1883 he entered the Law School of Trinity College and, as usual, appears to have worked very hard. In 1884 he took first prize in Civil Law, and in 1885 first prize in Feudal and English Law.

All these occurrences in his life were at a time of serious economic and political problems in the country. The interests and demands of academia could not disguise topics of general conversation, especially when they actively involved his father.

CHAPTER FIVE

Social and Political Mise en Scène

The year John entered Trinity College, 1879, was a disastrous year for Irish agriculture, the culmination of three bad years. Land agitation began in Mayo, and the Irish National Land League was founded with Parnell as president. On a more constructive note, the University Ireland Act was passed. The Queen's Colleges of Belfast, Cork and Galway became endowed colleges under a new examining university, the Royal University, which made university education and degrees readily available to Catholics. During the year, the major legal and political figure, Isaac Butt, died. The following year, Parnell, as leader of the Irish Parliamentary Party, addressed the United States House of Representatives in February, and at Ennis, in September, made his 'moral coventry' speech which led to the ostracism of Captain Boycott. The chief secretary, William E. Foster, proclaimed the Land League to be 'an unlawful criminal association', an action unlikely to have been taken without the approval of the powerful Master of the Rolls.

In 1881, a coercion bill was passed, and in August 1881 there was Gladstone's second Land Act, in which Edward Sullivan played a prominent role; and, on 13 October, Mr Sullivan pushed through the arrest of Parnell, which was followed in the next two days by the arrest of the other Land League leaders. In response, a No Rent manifesto was issued from Kilmainham Jail; and agrarian outrages grew in number and intensity.

During April 1882 negotiations took place with Parnell; and on 2 May the 'Kilmainham Treaty' was accepted by the cabinet: arrears in the rent question were settled, and the no-rent manifesto was withdrawn and effective efforts to stop outrages were promised. The fallout from the treaty, however, was considerable. Chief Secretary Foster resigned, as did Earl Cowper, the Viceroy. It was evidently a difficult period within the administration. It is not evident where Edward Sullivan stood. Wherever his sympathies lay, he did not resign and served under the new Lord Lieutenant, Earl Spencer. Then, to add a new dimension to the internal pressures, three days after the acceptance of the 'Kilmainham Treaty', the newly-appointed Chief Secretary, Lord Frederick Cavendish, and Thomas Burke, the Under-Secretary, were murdered in the Phoenix Park, Dublin. This occasioned widespread revulsion and condemnation. A crimes bill was introduced, and thorough efforts were made to trace the perpetrators.

For the benefit of the populace, meanwhile, St Stephen's Green had been opened to the public in 1880, and in August 1882 an Exhibition of Irish Arts and Manufacturers opened in Rotunda Hospital gardens, Dublin. One would hope that young Mr Sullivan took the time to explore both venues. In Trinity, interest was likely to have been aroused by the handing over to the Jesuits of the running of University College Dublin, the building in which Newman founded the Catholic University. John would certainly have been aware, too, of agitation in the Royal Irish Constabulary (RIC) over pay and conditions, resulting in a strike in the force in Limerick during August, while in Dublin discontent among the Dublin Metropolitan Police led to 500 men being dismissed. These developments were closely followed by his father, as were the developments in the case of the 'Invincibles', those responsible for the Phoenix Park murders.

Sentencing the Invincibles
On 13 January 1883, seventeen Irish Invincibles were arrested. Edward Sullivan and James Murphy determined to bring about convictions. Sullivan was said to have been the mainspring of the government in suppressing the Invincibles,[22] while Murphy, as crown prosecutor, achieved the breakthrough that connected the prisoners to the murders. One prisoner, Peter Carey, was in-

formed by the police officer on the case, Superintendent Mallon, that another prisoner had betrayed him, and this led to a breakdown in Carey's resistance and to his implicating the other prisoners. James Murphy trusted Mallon, visited Carey in his cell and took down his confession. That afternoon, Carey 'was in the box as a witness on behalf of the Crown'.[23]

Jubilation at the breakthrough was shared by the Sullivan and Murphy families. In later years, John Sullivan would enliven a long walk with stories of court cases he had witnessed or of cases and incidents described to him by his father. The Invincibles were tried before Judge William O'Brien, the third member of the triumvirate of friends. Between 14 May and 9 June, five men were executed: Joseph Brady, Daniel Curley, Timothy Kelly, Michael Fagan, and Thomas Caffrey. Others were sentenced to life imprisonment in Australia. Meantime, members of the dynamite campaign in Britain were arrested in London and Birmingham. The four men were sentenced to life imprisonment. One of them was Henry Wilson, alias Thomas J. Clarke, future leader of the 1916 insurrection.

Edward Sullivan believed in applying the law evenly. On 16 October 1881, at Rosslea, Co Fermanagh, there were rival meetings and a collision between nationalists and an Orange party that was led by Lord Rossmore, JP and Grand Master for Co Monaghan. Much of the precipitation came from Rossmore. Sullivan intervened firmly, and on 24 November Rossmore was suspended from the magistracy.[24]

In 1883, Sir Edward Sullivan was appointed Lord Chancellor. The following year he became disillusioned with Mr Gladstone's policies. He was concerned that the prime minister was embarked on acceding to the Irish nationalist demand for Home Rule. He was strongly opposed to such a measure, as were his two close friends, Judges O'Brien and Murphy. During his career he published a number of volumes of essays written in an effective but combative style, dealing with an unusual variety of subjects, from military reform to the use of farmyard manure. In 1884, in his final volume of essays entitled *Stray Shots*, he made a number of biting attacks on his political leader. The book opens with an introduction, which is a kind of political, economic and social profession of faith. Some of the professions of this creed have a counter-cultural ring, such as, 'I am in favour of female suffrage', and 'I believe that the distribution of wealth is of more importance than its accumulation', but when he comes to the issue of Home Rule he becomes almost strident.[25]

> I believe that Gladstoneism is the national enemy:
> I believe that Gladstoneism has made the Repeal of the
> Irish Union inevitable:
> That it has ruined Egypt:
> That it has unsettled India:
> That it has fanned class antipathies to a heat never
> before seen in this country:
> That it has everywhere brought the honour of England
> into contempt:
> That it is a policy of 'cant and re-cant':
> That it will ruin the Empire.

In nailing his colours so uncompromisingly to the mast, he was jeopardising his career. Knowing this must have greatly added to the many pressures inherent in his office as Lord Chancellor.

Edward Sullivan's grave misgivings about the effects of Gladstoneism were reinforced at the start of the New Year. On 21 January 1885, Parnell made the defiant pronouncement that 'no man has a right to fix the boundary to the march of a nation'; three days later there were dynamite explosions in Westminster Hall, the House of Commons, and the Tower of London; and on 26 January, Khartoum fell to the Mahdi's forces after a siege of 317 days and General Gordon was killed. A split occurred in the cabinet over the situation in Egypt and Sudan. Then on 23 March, presumably with Sullivan's legal advice and support, the Viceroy or Lord Lieutenant, Earl Spencer, put a memorandum to cabinet urging the replacement of the Crimes Act by strengthening the ordinary law of the United Kingdom, and introducing remedial measures for Ireland [that would help to counter crime and the demand for Home Rule] such as local government, land purchase, and the abolition of the viceroyalty.

In April, the Prince and Princess of Wales, the future King Edward and Queen Alexandria, came on a goodwill mission to Ireland. On Friday, 10 April, they laid the foundation-stones of the Science and Art Museum and the National Library of Ireland. The following day, there was a special banquet at Dublin Castle, and Edward Sullivan sat next to the Princess of Wales. Those who were present observed 'that he never appeared in better spirits and never displayed to greater effect those social talents which were not the least remarkable of the many brilliant qualities of his gifted nature'.[26] Two days later he was dead.

CHAPTER SIX

The Sudden Death of the Lord Chancellor

On the morning of 13 April he felt a slight pain, which grew worse in the afternoon. A doctor was summoned, but on arrival he found the Lord Chancellor dead, sitting in his armchair. He had suffered an aneurism of the aorta or main heart artery.

The *Freeman's Journal* of the following day told of the intense sensation created in many places by the news of his unexpected death. He was expected to have many more years in public life. 'No figure was better known in the city than his lithe, active form, and the quick step and alert and active carriage were those of a man on whom his sixty-two years sat very lightly.' The paper went on to recount the chancellor's many talents: 'a great orator, a most pugnacious leader, and a lawyer of vast erudition', he found his first interest as 'a man of Letters'. He was a warm family man, who never got over the death of his son. A loyal friend, he did not neglect his old intimates on his rising to power. 'In a country where advancement is too often disgraced by corruption and pomposity, it never changed in the slightest degree the manly nature, the frank bearing and kind heart of Sir Edward Sullivan.' It was not an occasion to speak of political issues, the paper observed, and then noted that politically he was in accord with popular views on many issues, especially religious equality, but did not understand or appreciate 'the great Irish movement of ancient days. He showed himself ready, however, to uphold the law against societies however "loyal" or offenders however highly placed'.[27]

The shock and upheaval for Lady Sullivan and her family must have been extreme. Edward Sullivan was such an active, dynamic, assertive personality that it was almost impossible to come to grips with his absence. John Sullivan was deeply affected and troubled by the suddenness of the death. He was the only one of the brothers to be living in Dublin, and had enjoyed contact with his father, listening to his experiences and benefiting from his 'well-stored mind'. He continued his studies and, as noted, obtained first prize in Feudal and English Law. This last had, perhaps, a special significance. He decided to leave Trinity College without finishing his degree and to study for the English bar at Lincoln's Inn. His abandonment of an Irish law degree was something, one feels sure, his father would not have condoned. John now felt free to make the decision, and he had been left sufficiently well off to be independent. But why the seemingly abrupt resolution with only a short time left before qualifying, and when his presence could have been a support to his mother?

Why Leave Trinity?

There is no clear answer. Later, he would say on different occasions how much he owed to the example and prayers of his mother, and he compared his situation to that of St Augustine and his mother, St Monica. There has never been any suggestion of sexual impropriety on the part of John Sullivan. There was, however, his reference to having stopped going to church while at Trinity. Authors have speculated on the negative influences of Professors Tyrell and Mahaffy, but as against that he greatly revered another classics professor, Lewis Purser, a former Portora student, whom he described years later as 'the most Christ-like man I ever met'.[28] Some clues to the reference to Augustine and a disordered lifestyle is tentatively suggested by an uncharacteristic review and more persuasively by a remark of his brother. The year John won his moderatorship and gold medal, the editor of the Trinity periodical devoted to classical studies, *Hermathena*, asked him to review the latest Oxford edition of Aeschylus' *Agamemnon* by A. S. Margoliouth, then a young fellow of New College, Oxford, later to be master of all Arabic studies and to be considered one of the most learned men in England. The shy and gentle John Sullivan gave the work a scathing review, pointing to misprints, wrong references, careless accentuation, and to 43 emendations claimed by Margoliouth for which he, Sullivan, was able to name earlier scholars.[29] The criticism was unrelieved, delivered with the insensitive omniscience of a recently successful graduate. It was a performance to embarrass an older John Sullivan.

The other possible clue was provided by Mathias Bodkin in his book *The Port of Tears*.[30] He described John Sullivan, an austere Jesuit in ancient, patched clothes, sitting at table in his brother William's club and crumbling some bread while he listened to his brother. 'Suddenly there entered the room a character well known for good living, hard drinking, and a robust contempt for clerics. Sir William raised a hand and called him to their table, where he stood in astonished and candid disgust at the unusual figure before him. "Don't you know my brother?" asked William. "Surely you do, surely you have not forgotten John? Many a time I've seen the pair of you on the top of a cab rolling home with the milk".' There was not a word from John. The other man, 'with brows black as thunder', denied the charge. It was not, Bodkin opined, that he resented a wild youth, but that he was associated with this shabby priest.

Bodkin dismissed, however, any possibility of John being so involved. But was he reading back into the past: conscious of the austere Fr Sullivan and judging any youthful wildness quite unthinkable in his regard? Why, after all, would William have called the man to their table, and stated so firmly that he had often seen the two of them coming home after a long night out? Some such indulgence and company makes sense of John's special need of his mother's prayers, and of his decision, following the shock of his father's death, not to finish his law degree and to leave Trinity and Dublin for a fresh start in England.

That there was a convivial and sociable side to John is well attested. Mary Hayden, professor of Irish History at University College Dublin – a graduate of the Royal University, which in 1884 produced the first women graduates in Ireland – recalled for some of her Jesuit students that she used to be invited by John Sullivan to join a coterie in his rooms to talk modern Greek and drink real Turkish coffee: 'He made it by a special rite of his own, and it was a great point with him.'[31] There is ample evidence, moreover, that then, or slightly later, he was a more than competent whist player. His brother William spoke of it after John's death, and a Mr A. W. Perry, of Rathdrum, Co Laois, who called on his friend Herbert Wilson in Trinity College, noted that a group of students used to meet in Wilson's rooms, where 'all learned their whist, and especially the art of finessing, from John Sullivan, who knew Cavendish from cover to cover.'[32] With his father's sudden death, however, and the resultant sense of the fragility and uncertainty of life, his manner of living, and the college's enclosed social circle, were no longer acceptable. He felt it necessary to cut the painter, to take the drastic step of not finishing his degree, and to seek the wider horizons and freedom of London.

CHAPTER SEVEN

In England and Abroad

Perry next met John Sullivan in 1885, when he was studying brewing at London University College. He found John very generous. He entertained Perry to dinner many times, in company with other students whose allowances were modest.

After two years in Lincoln's Inn, John qualified for the English bar. Thereafter, he seems never to have appeared in the English courts; but he worked in chambers with R. F. McSwinney, a well-known expert in mining law. He also obtained the post as marshal to Lord Chief Justice Mathew, which was a lucrative and valuable experience since the Chief Justice was one of the ablest lawyers of his generation.[33] According to Debrett for 1895, John's chambers were at 9 Old Square, Lincoln's Inn, WC, and he was a member of the Reform Club, then in its heyday.[34] During these years he had money to spend on clothes, meals and entertainment, and he had time and opportunity to embark on foreign travel. He did the usual continental trips, and also made walking tours in Greece, Macedonia and Asia Minor, visiting scenes made familiar to him from his classical studies.

An instance of his way of proceeding as a tourist was outlined by the same Mr Perry who had met him in Wilson's rooms in Trinity. In 1892, Perry was ordered to St Moritz to overcome his asthma. On his arrival, the first person he met was John Sullivan, 'who had just arrived after a tremendous journey on foot, alone, as usual, and carrying with him a towel, so that he might enjoy from time to time a plunge in the very cold Alpine lakes'. The Moritz Bad Hotel had just opened at the bottom of St Moritz, and John promptly invited his friend to dinner to mark the occasion.[35]

He was known to travel light – with a toothbrush, a couple of shirts, and a sleeping bag. In later years, on occasions when his reserve could be overcome, he would pour out a wealth of memories connected with his travels of which only fragments remain: his first impression of Greece in springtime – valley filled with the pink and white of peach and almond blossoms; his months in a monastery on Mount Athos, where the pilgrim arrived at the door in a basket, hauled up by rope; the bandit who accosted him in some lonely spot and whom he bought off with a packet of cigarettes; his visit to the Homeric Zakynthos, one of the Ionian islands most famously reigned over by Odysseus; and the *strategos* or mayor, bearing the Hellenic-sounding name Morfeos, who turned out to be a descendent of a remote Irish Murphy, whose wild-goose flight led him to this unexpected haven.[36]

John had a rare gift for making friends. In his travels, he met in Athens M. Tricoupis, the Prime Minister of Greece, who became an admirer. He introduced John to some notables as a young Irishman who could not only converse with them in modern Greek, but also in ancient Greek, 'which few of us can boast of being able to do'. His regard for the young Irishman led to his facilitating him in his travels and explorations, going so far, on at least one occasion, as to provide him with an escort of soldiers.[37]

John also proved popular in the austere environment of Mount Athos. His meditative, unassuming manner and basic simplicity appealed to a number of the monks, even though he was a Protestant. Carrie Otis-Cox, a niece of Judge William O'Brien, recalled instances of his capacity for making foreign friends. Around 1893, in Dublin, 'John Sullivan had a great friend, a Greek, or rather a Cyprian (*sic*), called Demetrius Yacovides, a young medical student at Trinity … They came to see us at Merrion Square. The contrast was striking between John's fair hair, blue eyes, and phlegmatic manner, and the young Greek's alive, pulsing personality. Mr Yacovides invited us to tea at his rooms. In those days young girls were not allowed the same liberty as today, but as John was to be there, my uncle decided it was all right … We were let go with John whenever the occasion presented itself … I can still see the old Merrion Square dining-room with its polished mahogany and silver, and John, quiet as the monks he was telling us about, reading extracts from the letters of his Mount Athos friends, with his friend, Demetrius Yacovides, looking at him in amused and friendly admiration. Those letters were from monks John had met at Mount Athos. They usually began by "My dearly beloved John", and had a religious trend and an intellectual flavour. They were to me reminiscent of the Epistles. I hope I did not titter as I listened, especially as John seemed to derive the greatest pleasure and satisfaction from them.' She also remembered him telling her and her sister 'of the strict Lenten fast at Mount Athos, and how, on the Easter festival, a gargantuan repast was offered to guests and visitors'.[38]

CHAPTER EIGHT

The Mount Athos Effect

The Mount Athos experience seems to have marked a turning-point in John Sullivan's life. The fact that he contemplated spending some time on the 'holy mountain' indicated that already he was in search of some spiritual reality. Two or three months endeavouring to live the monastic life, with its silence, its liturgies, singing or saying the psalms and rising at night to do so, the long Orthodox Masses, the periods of manual work, the severe fast during Lent, were bound to effect change in one who enters on the experience honestly and freely. It can bring a new spiritual depth, a healing of mind and spirit, which spotlights what is tawdry in one's life. It seems to have had such an effect on John. It also brought a desire to search for something similar in the western tradition.

This was heightened, perhaps, by an infection he contracted on his way back from Greece. He made his way to London and was staying at the Reform Club with his brother, Edward, when he became seriously ill. Dr Mapother, a well-known Dublin surgeon who had settled in London, was summoned. He diagnosed smallpox, and had the patient removed to what was then the Highgate Smallpox Hospital. He was well looked after there, but he used to recall in later years that the only precautions against infection taken by the doctor were to wear a mackintosh and to stand at the end of the bed. The illness was a light one, and had no serious after-effects.[39] It was a lonely time of isolation, nevertheless, and Judge O'Brien used to express the view that it must have been during that time that he made up his mind to enter the Catholic Church.[40]

There is no direct evidence to support this, but after the

Mount Athos experience his interest in religion is noted, and a rather abstracted manner which marked him as apart, though not aloof. Carrie Otis-Cox commented on 'his strange far-away expression, albeit he was quite alive to what was going on and what was said'. Around this time, 1893, her uncle 'often mentioned that John was looking worried and absent-minded, and he wondered if it was his health, or if he were contemplating becoming a Catholic'. He mentioned this last 'in a tone of awe'.[41] Such a step was not to be taken lightly. The social consequences could be considerable. Many people would be upset, including relations and friends.

It seems to have been in this period that he expanded his interest in spiritual reading, and developed a special admiration for St Francis of Assisi. He also spoke with Judge Murphy about alms-giving and concern for the poor, and he always remembered the judge's advice that more important than giving money to a poor man was to relate to him personally as a human being. It was said of Murphy that 'he was unusual in that he was not spoiled by his elevation to the bench ... One of the most pugnacious of counsel, he was transformed into the most genial of judges'.[42]

CHAPTER NINE

Enjoying the Social Scene

Despite the new seriousness and his aloofness in manner, John Sullivan remained active in society and good company. Something of the social round in those years was conveyed by Carrie Otis-Cox much later in the course of an article published in a *Le Havre* newspaper. She and her sister were American, but settled in France.

> Life was carefree and pleasant then in the Irish capital. I recall the miniature court where a viceroy reigned, aristocratic ballrooms where one danced to the strains of a military band, artistic and literary circles, dinners at which the Catholic bishop sat beside the Protestant chaplain, equal in society, but as yet unequal before the law, the famous horse-races at Punchestown and Leopardstown, the regattas of the St George Yacht Club, parties at Howth and Killiney, all that dream world of half a century ago.

On her own admission elsewhere, her uncle gave permission for many such outings because John Sullivan was with her and her sister; and she also recalled 'what delightful walks we had with him over the violet heather that clothes the Wicklow mountains'.[43] Both girls were very much at home with him and used to tell him 'what they thought about everyone and everything'. When he brought them to the zoo, he enjoyed the game they began to play – finding resemblances between certain animals and different people they knew. He had brought good quality biscuits for the animals, and the girls began to eat them for themselves. This created a problem. As much of their time was spent in France, they wore veils French fashion that were gathered under the chin and tied behind the head. It was virtually impossible to raise them to eat the biscuits. Having failed in their initial efforts, John lent a hand and made matters worse if anything, and mumbled to his own amusement that it was like one of Cervantes' heroes whose helmet had to be raised so that he could be fed!

Another day they went on a long walk to Sandymount, where the girls collected some sea-shells, and then had a rather rushed walk all the way to Lady Sullivan's house where they were to take tea.

> Tea at Lady Sullivan's used to be great fun, and Annie was very lively and always knew the latest news or gossip. John used to sit on the sofa, his cup of tea in his hand, and listen with a bored expression, although highly amused at all our nonsense. He could not help his expression, it was natural.[44]

At that period, he was worried about his health, and would eat no bread except Hovis, which was in vogue at the time. 'His complexion had a peculiar hue, which my uncle called autumn leaf, and his hands were such a deep red as to be nearly blue. One could not help noticing them, especially as he had a trick of passing his hand through his thick hair, which, added to his general expression, would have given him a bored and worried look were it not for the genial smile with which he greeted friends.'[45]

One of John's favourite places to visit was Glencairn, Murphy's residence, later the abode of the Boss Croker of Tamany Hall, where the Derby winner, Orby, was partly trained. Jessica Murphy, a daughter of the judge, observed: 'My father was devoted to John Sullivan, and enjoyed his deep classical and literary knowledge. It was generally on Sundays that he came to us ... He never joined in our outdoor games – I fancy he was delicate, though a good walker. He was initially shy and reserved, and he rarely lifted his beautiful blue eyes and looked one straight in the face, but when he began to talk he was always interesting'. She remembered his description of the monastery on Mount Athos. Her brother, Edward, who became the Lord Justice of Appeal in Northern Ireland, confirmed that John was rather shy and retiring and that all the members of the Murphy family were fond of him. 'As I was following in my father's footsteps', Edward explained, 'so far as a classical education was concerned, John seemed to take a special interest in me, and often talked about passages in Greek or Roman authors with me, whilst at other times he talked of English poetry. I can recall his appreciation of the "Bridge of Sighs" with its lovely concluding words. I would describe him as a man of great taste in English literature and the classics, serious-minded, somewhat shy, and always most kindly, especially to young people'.[46] The 'Bridge of Sighs', which seldom features in modern anthologies, was by Thomas Hood, the theme was a young woman who drowned herself, and the 'lovely concluding words' were:

Owning her weakness,
Her evil behaviour,
And leaving with meekness
Her sins to her Saviour!

It has been said that 'no poem shows the shift in language, mores and taste from early Victorian to current times any better than Thomas Hood's "The Bridge of Sighs".'[47] It is interesting to note that John Sullivan seemed to have become part of that shift in language, mores and taste by the 1890s

Walking and cycling were John's favourite relaxations. In the 1890s, in which so much change flourished, cycling became popular, especially with the development of the pneumatic tyre. The manufacturers could not keep up with the demand. Groups of men and women cycled into the countryside or along the coast roads, stopping perhaps to enjoy the scenery or for a picnic or snack. A Mrs Maguire remembered setting out as a young woman on such a picnic with a number of young friends including John Sullivan; and she recalled how as they rode along the Stillorgan Road, then in completely rural surroundings, John was out in front, 'his fair hair flying in the breeze', whilst the young women of the party begged him to go slower'.[48]

Thus, in the 1890s, John Sullivan was popular, likeable, highly respected, well off, and known, in Fr Tom Finlay's words, as 'the best dressed young man in Dublin'. Not surprisingly, therefore, he was, as Carrie Otis-Cox put it, 'a catch in the matrimonial market, and his sister, to whom he was the apple of her eye, was not slow to perceive the enemy's attack from whatever quarter it came'. She called to mind 'a big dinner party' at which she, her sister, John and Annie were guests. 'With veiled, but clear intention, he had been seated next to an ambitious mother, who dreamed of him for a son-in-law. Annie Sullivan came to see us the next day to talk over the dinner. "Did you see how nicely John was pinned?" were her very first words.'[49]

CHAPTER TEN

Intimations of Change

Although John Sullivan, in the first half of the 1890s, seemed to Carrie Otis-Cox 'to have no definite religious views', a great deal was going on within. He had discovered St Augustine's *Confessions*, and was deeply moved. He found similarities between his own and Augustine's early scepticism, and he was conscious of his Catholic mother praying for him as Monica had for her son, and how they shared a febrile restlessness in search of meaning and truth, and he was drawn to Augustine's conclusion – 'You have made us for yourself, O Lord, and we can never rest until we rest in Thee.' A gradual curiosity about Catholicism began to assert itself. An unusual instance of this was mentioned by a Mrs Esther O'Kiely, wife of Professor O'Kiely of University College Dublin.

In 1894 and 1895, when she was a little girl in her parents' Glencar Hotel, Co Kerry, John Sullivan stayed there. She used to be instructed by her governess near an open window that looked out on the front garden. One rather cold summer's morning, Mr Sullivan stood on the gravel outside the window wearing a grey tweed suit, his trousers pulled up beyond his knees, and no shoes or stockings. The lesson was from the Catholic catechism, and on seeing him the governess ceased the instruction because she knew he was a Protestant. He asked the little girl what she was learning. She told him it was the catechism. He asked if he might listen to the instruction. First he had a look at *Butler's Catechism*, then handing back the little book he sat on the window-sill and listened to the lesson. When the lesson was finished, he asked Esther if he might take the book until the evening, and if he might come next morning to hear the instruction again.

Next morning John came to the classroom and asked the governess if she would continue the catechism lesson. He listened
and asked questions. Esther was doing some bible history, too,
and he took the name of the book, saying he would get one for
himself and a catechism so that next year he would be able to
follow the instructions more clearly. Next year, he brought with
him a book on *The Lives of the Saints*, but insisted on hearing the
catechism lesson right through. 'He used to inquire a good deal
about Confession and the Mass. He did go to Mass while at our
place, but never showed any anxiety to meet the local clergy.'
'He used to go for long walks, generally off the road, by river,
lake or mountain. He was a rather silent man, not anxious to
gossip.'

John came only twice to Glencar, but for many years he sent
Esther a book for Christmas, always a book with some religious
stories when she would have preferred something like
Chatterbox. She lost contact with him when she went to boarding
school. Then in 1906 she got a personal message from him. A
young Jesuit student, visiting his family in the neighbourhood,
brought kind remembrances from Mr Sullivan and the news
that he was going to be a priest.[50]

The only other clue as to what was going on in the inner life
of this very private man came through another young girl. Mrs
Isabella M. Cummins, proprietress of a private hotel in Leeson
Street, Dublin, came across Mr Sullivan when she was aged
about twelve and went to pray at a house in Cork Street for a
friend of her grandparents, a Mr Thomas O'Grady. He had died
in St Mary's Hospice (Our Lady's Hospice, Harold's Cross) and
was brought home in preparation for the funeral. She knelt by
the bed and said what prayers she knew for the dead. Then she
noticed that a very well dressed man had come in and was
standing in a corner of the room. Her eyes were drawn to his
black walking-stick with a silver knob – known as 'a dandy
stick' and later seen only on the stage. His hands were resting on
the top of the stick and he appeared to be praying for the dead
man. When she got up from her knees and went to leave, he

asked her name and where she went to school, and then asked her to say a prayer for him as she had prayed for Mr O'Grady. Child-like, she responded: 'These were dead prayers. I cannot say them for you.' He replied: 'Then say some live prayers for me.' She held up three fingers and promised: 'I will say three Hail Marys for you. They are live prayers.'

Some time later, while she was at school at the Mercy Convent School, Brickfield Lane, she was called out of class and brought over to the convent to Sr Mary Stanislaus Joseph, who introduced her to her friend Miss Annie Sullivan, and with her was her brother, Mr John Sullivan who, presumably, had asked to see her.

In those years, John was a frequent visitor to patients in Our Lady's Hospice (St Mary's Hospice), often bringing presents to cheer people who were feeling low. He had been visiting Thomas O'Grady there, which explained his presence in the house in Cork Street.[51] For all his capacity for expeditions on his own, he was discovering what the mystics had always said, that the Christian must follow the difficult path of moving beyond self and self-sufficiency.

CHAPTER ELEVEN

Public and Political Interests, and Conversion

John Sullivan in later life was thought to be completely removed from the world and national events, and this surmise was thought to apply generally to his life. As has been indicated, it is most unlikely that a member of the Sullivan family could be un-affected by public events. One former student of Fr Sullivan in Clongowes recalled the enthusiasm with which he spoke of the Liberal MP, Henry Campbell Bannerman, leaving his listeners with the impression that he knew the man personally. This last seems quite likely. Campbell Bannerman, a follower of Gladstone, was well known to John's father and was also a classical scholar – a passport to wide links. In the years between 1885 and 1896 John made numerous friends in Britain, among them politicians from the main parties. Campbell Bannerman led the Liberal party in opposition, after Gladstone's resignation in 1894; and he was highly regarded as the man who kept the party together until forced by ill-health to hand over to Asquith in 1908. That John's contacts also extended to Conservatives, and that he was esteemed as a man of ability, experience and judgement, was in-dicated by his appointment by the Conservative government in 1895 to a commission to investigate the widespread massacre of Armenians at Adana in Asia Minor. It was a situation that was generating public attention and anger. The Christian Armenians had been persecuted frequently during the nineteenth century under the Muslim-controlled Ottoman Empire. In 1895 revolts took place among the Armenian subjects of the empire, and the Sultan Abdul Hamid is said to have decided to massacre tens of thousands of Armenians in what became known as the Hamidian massacres. The indignation felt in western Europe led to the establishment of the commission. That it effected little of lasting effect was demonstrated by further massacres in 1908, and above all during the First World War, when up to 1.5 million were reported brutally killed.

John had much to arouse his interest in Ireland, too, in the years after his father's death. The defeat of Gladstone's Home Rule Bill in 1886 was followed by the Plan of Campaign against excessive rents and the *Times* publication of letters, purportedly from Parnell, supporting public crime, including the Phoenix Park murders. Parnell's challenge of the newspaper in a dramatic trial caught the interest not only of politicians, and John's legal circle in London, but of the public generally. The discrediting of Richard Pigott as the forger, which was greatly aided by the evidence of Dr Walsh, the very able Catholic Archbishop of Dublin, led to the full justification of Parnell. He was at a crest of popularity in Britain and Ireland when the O'Shea divorce case was introduced. Again, there was a period of prolonged public drama that captured the public interest. When Parnell did not defend the case, Gladstone called for his resignation, the Irish Parliamentary Party split, and in subsequent bitter election campaigns Parnell lost seats and undermined his health. His death came suddenly in October 1891. His funeral was the largest seen in Dublin up to that time. The split over the divorce issue and Gladstone's call for his resignation left an indelible scar in Irish political memory, and John Sullivan with his numerous legal and political connections, and his family history, could not have remained unaffected. The Irish question continued to hold attention in Britain and Ireland as Gladstone pursued Home Rule, had his third Home Rule Bill passed in the House of Commons, only to be defeated by the Lords. He resigned the following year and, as Campbell Bannerman sought to hold a divided Liberal party together, power passed to the Conservatives under Lord Rosebery.

As a literary man, there was also much to interest John Sullivan. Apart from the commencement of the Irish Literary Movement, and the Irish Language Movement, there was the death of Alfred Lord Tennyson in 1892 and his burial in

Westminster Abbey; and it would be surprising if he did not attend in February 1895 the first public performance of the much acclaimed *Importance of being Earnest* by the old Portoran and Trinity playwright and wit, Oscar Wilde. Two months later, in another dramatic trial that caught public attention, Wilde was found guilty at the Old Bailey of homosexual offences and sentenced to two years hard labour. One wonders if John Sullivan viewed his crime and suffering with the sympathy shown for the public offence and suffering of the woman in 'The Bridge of Sighs'.

Conversion and reaction

In the following year, 1896, there occurred the historic Locomotives Act, which permitted the practical use of motor cars on public roads. It was the kind of development that might be expected to greatly interest the fashionable John Sullivan; but it probably did not receive his active attention. For 1896 was the year, after lengthy consideration, in which he was received into the Catholic Church by Fr Michael Gavin SJ, at the Jesuit church, Farm Street, London.

The news of his conversion caused quite a stir in Dublin. It was well received by Catholic friends and acquaintances, but some of the Protestant community were angry. Close Church of Ireland friends, such as the Murphys, however, remained supportive. Judge James Murphy, indeed, gave the perfect answer to an indignant Presbyterian who accosted him with the words: 'Did you hear that your friend, John Sullivan, has become a Catholic?' To which the judge replied: 'Don't worry. John Sullivan would go to heaven even if he became a Presbyterian.'[52] His continued high esteem of John was further emphasised when his own son hesitatingly approached him about John's change of allegiance, expecting a strong condemnation. 'If John Sullivan has become a Catholic', was the reply, 'we may all consider whether we might not be well advised to do likewise.'[53] John was thirty-six years of age, half way through his life.

PART II

A Determined Change of Life and of Lifestyle

CHAPTER TWELVE

The First Change of Lifestyle

At the Hospice which he had attended, and in convents to which he was introduced by his sister, many of the nuns were impressed by his gentle, unassuming manner and had prayed for his conversion. He took his new commitment very seriously. His mother's companion, Miss O'Neill, observed that, on his return to Ireland after his reception into the Catholic Church, he went into his room and stripped it of everything that might appear luxurious, contenting himself with the plainest furniture and a carpetless floor. He had been fastidious about his dress. Now he changed to less expensive clothes, his silk underwear was replaced by ordinary linen, and his supply of carefully chosen ties was reduced from a couple of dozen to a few of the plainest pattern.[54] The 'poor man of Assisi' was a model much in mind. He became a regular visitor to the Capuchin friary at Church Street.

At the Hospice it was noted that he had a particular gift for putting the patients into good humour, and showed special sympathy towards the old, bringing them tins of snuff or packages of tea, and reading for them from religious books. The sisters observed that not only was there no side to him, there was a simplicity and straightforwardness that seemed to preclude concern about human respect. This was reflected in his approaching two young girls to learn the catechism with one and to ask the prayers of the other, and in his coming to the Hospice carrying under his arm for some patient a pair of boots, which he made no effort to cover in brown paper.[55]

A visitor of convents

He visited many convents, feeling at home in the atmosphere of work and prayer and making many friends. Among these locations were the Children's Hospital, Cappagh, on the outskirts of Dublin, and the schools attached to it. He was especially attracted to the Night School, which was conducted for the benefit of poor children who were employed during the day. The poorest of the children included two girls named Burke, who were particularly hard to manage. During the day they made their living as flower vendors and on one occasion were caught selling flowers in some location forbidden by law and were arrested. The next night, Sr Francesca, who was teaching in the school, told him of the arrest of the two girls. He immediately said, 'I'll see about that.' On the following night the girls reappeared and announced 'The Gentleman got us out.' He also came to the rescue of the Night Refuge, run by the Sisters of Mercy, in Brickfield Lane, to which were attached elementary schools. The superioress, in 1898, was in difficulties for a sum of £40 due to pay for bread for the Refuge. A Carmelite priest said he knew someone who could help. A few days later a young man handed in an envelope with £25 in banknotes and disappeared. This happened again, only this time his identity was revealed. He was invited in, and the doors were locked until the Sister Secretary had a chance to meet him and to thank him. From then on, he frequently visited the community. The nuns soon became aware that he had attained a considerable depth of spirituality. His conversation was almost entirely confined to spiritual topics, and he seemed to be very familiar with the works of St Teresa and St John of the Cross. The superioress used to bring the Sister Secretary to assist her to cope with the spiritual level of the conversation. By then, he was thinking about becoming a priest and mentioned or hinted it to the nuns. They prayed for him, and advised him to become a Jesuit.

John visited convents not only in Dublin, but throughout the country. He used to stay with his brother William frequently, when he was resident Magistrate for Cavan. While there, the Mother Abbess of the Poor Clare Convent, Ballyjamesduff, Mother Leontia Callen, became a good friend. He confided to her that he intended entering a religious order. She assured him that his vocation was for the Society of Jesus. He cycled to Mass in the convent when Mass was not available in the parish church, but never used the prie-dieu left for him but knelt on the floor. His appearance even then was edifying and austere. One day at recreation, a sister remarked that Mr Sullivan was very holy looking. 'Holy looking', an elderly sister exclaimed, 'why you could light a candle before him!'

He was ready to help the nuns in any way he could. A striking instance of this was at a convent in Cork to which he travelled to attend the devotion known as the Forty Hours Adoration before the Blessed Sacrament, and pontifical High Mass celebrated by the bishop. On his arrival he found the nuns vainly trying to cope with their ordinary work and getting the chapel ready for the morrow's ceremony. The Reverend Mother remarked to him that she feared that things would never be ready. He told her to put the sisters back at their ordinary tasks, he would look after the chapel himself. Single-handed, he moved the benches, got bucket and mop and brush, and swept and scrubbed and polished the chapel. It was late at night when he was finished, and by then his clothes were showing the effect of the day's work. He knelt down at the back of the chapel and, it would appear, spent the rest of the night in prayer until the Mass began.

After the Mass next morning, the bishop and Fr Peter Finlay, professor of theology at the Jesuit theologate, Milltown Park, Dublin, who narrated this incident, were standing on the steps outside the chapel when John Sullivan emerged. When he saw the bishop, he came up to kiss his ring and then slipped away. The bishop turned to Fr Finlay and remarked that he thought it very imprudent of the Reverend Mother to allow ragged fellows like that to be about the premises. 'My Lord', said Fr Finlay in a dryly humorous tone, 'that is the Lord Chancellor's son.'[56] It was Peter Finlay's more famous brother, Tom, Professor of Economics at University College Dublin and co-founder of the Irish Cooperative Movement, who had previously described John as 'the best-dressed young man in Dublin'.

The Passing of a friend and of his mother

In these years, also, John acted as registrar to Judge William O'Brien, with whom he appeared in the law courts at Cork, Limerick, Killarney, Carlow, and Naas. As they travelled by train they had ample opportunity to discuss many things, including their common literary interests. William O'Brien, like John's father, was a collector of rare books and documents. He amassed a remarkable library, containing several early Shakespeare folios and some 150 incunabula. These treasures he bequeathed to the library of the Jesuit theologate at Milltown Park.[57] He was also a frequenter of convents in the course of his circuit. He brought John to some of them, including that of the Poor Clare Colletines in Carlow where he introduced him as being 'greatly interested in nuns'.[58]

In 1898 Lady Sullivan died. Little is known about her death, whether it was sudden or the result of an illness. All that is recorded is the comment of a third party that John's regard for his mother was indicated at the funeral when he placed a bunch of lilies on the coffin as it was lowered into the grave. As mentioned already, he paid tribute on a number of occasions to the importance to him of the example of her life, her faith and prayerfulness. With her death, home was no longer the same. Any ties delaying his response to a life in religion were largely dissipated.

Already, his inner change was manifested in outward behaviour. On 1 January 1899, Judge O'Brien wrote to his sister, Mrs John Otis-Cox, residing in France: 'Mr John Sullivan is in the country. He is become quite a saint, and is an example to all people of religion and grace in conduct and manners.'[59] Later that year, the judge died. His niece, Carrie Otis-Cox, came to Ireland a day before his death. Mass was said in the bedroom of his house in Merrion Square, where her uncle lay in the habit of the Third Order of St Francis. She and John knelt and said the rosary beside the bed. She was struck 'how much older, and especially how changed' John looked. He served at the Mass and received Holy Communion, and she remembered being impressed 'by his fervour and saintly look and demeanour'. She added:

> After the funeral John came to see me. We sat in the same
> mahogany-furnished dining-room. The house had never
> been cheerful or comfortable, and it was ghastly that day.
> John was kind and thoughtful and friendly. I had never
> seen death before, and the loneliness of it all was a shock
> to me. We had had such a sheltered, united life. I think I
> made some remark about my uncle being so terribly
> alone, and I seem, even now, to hear John say, 'The dear
> Judge will be remembered where it is worth being re-
> membered', and I know he alluded to the Masses and
> prayers that would be said for him everywhere.

She never saw John Sullivan again. A year later he wrote to
her, 'enclosing two religious pictures' and telling her 'he was entering the Society of Jesus'.[60]

Entering the Jesuits was not as sombre as the foregoing
might suggest. It was preceded, in July 1890, by a festive visit to
the Poor Clares in Carlow, to whom he had been introduced by
the Judge. The sisters had moved to a new convent and he came
to Carlow to celebrate with them. He served four Masses in the
old parish church, and presented the sisters with a gold ciborium
and a sacristan's manual. There was an unconscious irony about
the latter gift. The sacristan was a precise and blunt lady who
corrected the eminent lawyer-acolyte for a breach of rubrics.
When reproached by her superior, she replied that there was no
harm done since 'Mr Sullivan was as humble as a child, and easier to manage than many an altar-boy.'[61] It was a fitting introduction to life in a Jesuit novitiate.

Just a few weeks after the ceremony in Carlow, Annie
Sullivan came in jubilation to the convent in Brickfield Lane,
Dublin, to announce that John had shaved off his moustache,
and was going to the Jesuit novitiate at Tullabeg, Co Offaly. He
came later himself to say goodbye, and seemed depressed. He
was saying goodbye to the independence of a professional man,
to the warmth of family and friends. At nearly forty years of age,

and only four years in the Catholic Church, it was a momentous step.[62]

Why the Jesuits? He had been attracted to the Capuchins and had a deep devotion to St Francis of Assisi. One surmises that he was influenced by the Jesuits who visited his home, or/and by those he met in Farm Street, and by the fact that so many of his nun friends told him he should join the Society of Jesus. He later observed that teaching young people was one of the greatest vocations, a belief that might well have influenced his choice. Ultimately, as with many major decisions in life, a variety of considerations probably combined to evoke the final decision.

CHAPTER THIRTEEN

Noviceship to Ordination

The Novitiate

The Jesuit novitiate at St Stanislaus College, Tullabeg, was situated some seven miles from the midlands town of Tullamore, Co Offaly, known then as Queen's County, in a countryside of drumlins and bogland. The main aim of the novitiate was to lead the novices to a strong personal devotion to Jesus Christ, and the main instrument in this process was a thirty-day retreat, further fostered by a routine which included daily Mass and fairly long periods of meditation, spiritual reading – including the classic work by Alphonsus Rodriguez, *The Practice of Christian and Religious Perfection*, which was to remain part of the staple diet of novices in many religious congregations into the 1960s, and regular exhortations on the Jesuit rule and ethos. Such intensive preparation, in an atmosphere of silence except for necessary communications which were to be made in Latin, with breaks for relaxation and periods of outdoor and indoor manual work, occupied the daily life of the novice for two years. When John's brother called to see him, he found 'the son of the Lord Chancellor' with a hoe scuffing the gravel before the house.

As the Jesuit order's constitutions envisaged a body of mobile, flexible men, free of the traditional demands of choir and cloister, and the fixed routines of older orders, Jesuit documents, and generations of novice masters, placed particular emphasis on personal prayer, self-discipline, obedience, and detachment or inner freedom. The groundwork of prayer was laid from the first days in the noviceship, and especially by means of the aforementioned long retreat – which was based on a short book by the order's founder, St Ignatius Loyola, which he entitled *Spiritual Exercises*, meaning by that something which leads to spiritual health and strength, analogous to physical exercises which induce health and strength of body, and which involved various forms of prayer, reflection on the gospel, and examination of conscience, and 'disposed the retreatant to rid himself (herself) of all inordinate attachments and to discover God's will in his/her regard'.

The Long Retreat and spiritual exercises
The long retreat of thirty days of silence, lectures, prayer and penances, opened with a consideration of the mysteries of creation and of sin as they related to the retreatant's own life and failings, and led on to a sense of gratitude to God and to an openness to his love and values as reflected in the gospel scenes of the life, death and resurrection of Jesus Christ. The intense, protracted, deeply personal involvement guided the novice towards inner freedom, or detachment, in decision making, and towards a frame of mind which sought God in all situations, circumstances and persons. John and his companions, like numerous men and women from the time of Ignatius to the present, were powerfully influenced and modified by the experience.

Detailed rules and customs further inculcated detachment and obedience, and humility was thought to be exercised by obeying fellow-novices who were put in charge of indoor or outdoor works, and by enduring a 'quarter of charity' in which, in the presence of the Master of Novices, one's fellow novices mentioned publicly one's failings for one's improvement. One day in the week was a villa day or holiday from lectures, when novices made sandwiches and set out in twos for a long walk. One's companion was allotted to one, to ensure equality, avoid favouritism, and practise detachment. There was also a time for team games, something that must have been particularly trying for John Sullivan.

For a man of forty years it must all have been very difficult. The novitiate consisted of first year and second year novices. In his first year, there was a total of 17 scholastic novices, that is novices destined for the priesthood, and 5 coadjutor novices, who aimed to become Religious Brothers in the Society of Jesus. In his second year, there was a larger entry into first year, which brought the total to 23 scholastic novices. Of the total scholastic novices, one was aged 24, John was 39, and all the others ranged from 16-19 years of age. As a result, the only one with whom he could confer on adult terms was the Master of Novices. Yet John sought to adapt with his customary thoroughness and with considerable success, even in his speaking of Latin. At certain times of the day, the novices were obliged to speak Latin, partly with a view to preparing them for later studies and lectures in that language. The standard of Latin of many novices was poor. John hid his own Ciceronian Latin under a form of bog Latin, using phrases like *omne recte* for 'all right', which led to some of the more proficient fellow novices to consider him something of a duffer. Nearly all, however, came to recognise his prayerfulness, his charity and kindness, and his spirit of penance. During one winter the joints of his fingers got very badly cracked and bled profusely. He refused to put anything on them to heal them.

St Ignatius had recommended that conversation should be of spiritual things. John took this very literally. He had developed an acute sense of sin, and his conversation was frequently of sin and death, of St Augustine and the prayer of St Monica in bringing about his conversion, and the lives of saints who were martyred for their belief. Some of his companions, as a result, found his conversation over-serious and even depressing. Fr Ernest Mackey, celebrated for his capacity to relate to and challenge boys and young men, remarked bluntly, if exaggeratedly, of his fellow-novice: 'All hated to be with him. Melancholy. His conversation was always gloomy holiness.' 'He had a Christ-like sympathy with all kinds of suffering combined with austerity. He was always talking of penitent saints, and seemed to have an amazing sense of sin. This may have explained his sadness.' 'He had a positive hero-worship for Fr Michael Browne.'[63]

Father Michael Browne

John's novice master, Michael Browne, was known as 'the saint' from early in his religious life. A classical scholar, he was a man of prayer, who sought to preserve recollection by keeping his eyes almost continuously lowered. His abstemiousness as regards food was proverbial. John received great assistance and assurance from Michael Browne when he was tempted to leave the noviceship. To Fr Browne's niece, Dorothy Browne, John wrote on 11 January 1932: 'I owe an immensity (*sic*) to the tenderness and charity of Father Michael Browne SJ. I don't think I could ever have persevered only for his unceasing sympathy and encouragement.'[64] Fr Fergal McGrath, who wrote the first account of Fr John Sullivan's career, conveyed John's reverence for Michael Browne in an instance from his own experience. At a special dinner in the noviceship on the Feast of St Stanislaus Kostka (a young Polish Jesuit, 1550-1568), on 13 November, Fergal, a novice, was sitting alongside Fr Sullivan, who ate nothing except a small portion of a bread roll, which he crumbled all over the table. On Fr Sullivan's other side was sitting an elderly Father who, towards the end of dinner, getting tired of fruitlessly passing on dish after dish, remarked reproachfully, 'You are a regular Father Michael Browne!' To which John replied in an earnest and embarrassed way: 'I wish I were, I wish I were'.[65]

Michael Browne, according to his biographer,[66] was usually serene and cheerful, but his judgement as Master of Novices was questioned by some in his allowing indiscreet penances, premature mysticism, and excessive asceticism (novices competing to eat less).[67] For him 'prayer was everything and the necessity of self-denial, humility and obedience in everything'.[68] His novices were conscious of his burning devotion to Christ, which he sought to reflect by severe bodily penances.[69] The care of the sick poor was a feature of his life, and in this too John Sullivan was his imitator.

Michael Browne and John Sullivan had strong scriptural support for abstemiousness and physical penance. Prayer and penance were also a feature of Christian life from early times. Problems arose in cases where fasting and penance were seen as good in themselves, and the body as something to be suppressed. The Greek depiction of a division between body and spirit, a dualism in which the body was viewed as a restriction almost a prison of the spirit, led readily to the practice of punishing the body, curbing its appetites by fasting, chains, flagellation, and other means. The attitude of mind that justified such practices found additional support in Calvinism, Jansenism, and the moral rectitude of Victorian times. In the Society of Jesus, especially in France, the attitude was to be found in such as Fr Gighnac, whose biography was translated into English by Fr Willie Doyle. Fathers Michael Browne, Willie Doyle, and John Sullivan reflected a prevailing spirituality of their time.

It required the development of the psychological sciences, and of scriptural scholarship, to bring about a more friendly attitude to the body, and an awareness that the Hebrew view of body and spirit was holistic – body and spirit made up the unity of the whole person, and was quite different from the dualism of the Greeks. Hence, 'to love one's neighbour as oneself' took on a different significance.[70]

Michael Browne outlived John Sullivan. After the latter's death, he spoke of his extraordinary simplicity and the objection which he had to speaking of himself or of his interesting travels, unless closely questioned. Already in the noviceship his great kindness showed itself. 'There was one novice who used to suffer from terrible desolation, and the only one who could always console him was Brother John Sullivan.'

On 8 September 1902, John took his first vows in the Society of Jesus in the domestic chapel in Tullabeg. On such occasions, to mark the event each new 'scholastic' (as the Jesuit student was now termed) was given a special crucifix. John had brought his mother's crucifix with him to the novitiate. He obtained permission from Fr Browne to take it as his vow crucifix. This brass crucifix, some 9 inches high, he carried with him all through his life and blessed countless people with it.

While the novices were cut off from newspapers and the news of the wider world, the Boer War was being waged and evoking much discussion and criticism in Ireland, and Queen

Victoria had come in a final visit to Dublin amid scenes of much enthusiasm and some opposition. For John, the emergence into the glare of ordinary life took on a special dimension. He was appointed not to any place in Ireland, but to Stonyhurst in Lancashire. While his fellow novices went to University College Dublin to take an Arts or Science degree, he, having university qualifications already, moved on to the next stage in the training process, namely, philosophical studies.

Taking Philosophy at Stonyhurst
He spent two years at St Mary's Hall, Stonyhurst, the philosophical seminary for the scholastics of the English province. In addition to lectures and study, there were rules and customs to be learned and followed, and there was a daily attendance at Mass, periods of meditation, a quarter of an hour 'examination of conscience' or prayerful review, twice a day. Once a year all did an eight-days retreat. John was the oldest of the scholastics.

Once he arrived, he found himself once more virtually cut off from outsiders. Information about him comes from fellow Jesuits, often the sharpest critics, because life in religion is led so much in common and the smallest foibles rapidly become evident. A man's goodness had to be genuine and constant to merit praise or even notice. Of the impression made by John Sullivan there seems little doubt. The available comments of contemporaries make this clear. To take just some of them:

Fr Patrick Nolan SJ, who came to Stonyhurst as a scholastic when John had completed the first year of his philosophy course, recalled that when he first met him, in September 1903, he 'was not much impressed, for he was a man who had no showy qualities'. Nolan continued:

> He seemed to my unpenetrating mind almost apologetic for his very existence … He was ever … diffident, utterly unpretentious, with a regular genius for depreciating himself before others. He spoke openly of his difficulties in his studies, and of the wonderful ability of some of his boyish companions, so much so that we young fellows,

thinking too much of ourselves, took him at his own valu-
ation. But ... some who were better able to judge soon de-
tected his fine knowledge of the classics, and observed
that though he was no master of the syllogism, he had a
thorough grasp of the Ethics course.

As he did not take part in our games, he was cut off
from many of us, but we met him on the 'walk days' and
came to know him better and, before the year was out, he
had won a place in all our hearts. He was very fond of
long walks and, on setting out, he let others talk. On the
return journey, when bodily fatigue made us silent, he,
tireless in mind and body, tried to entertain us, pouring
out a wealth of conversation ... enlivened by a sparkling
humour, which was all the more entertaining because we
had never supposed that he had that gift.

His unselfishness and thought for others were remarkable.

Despite his forty years of age, 'he was the first to volunteer
for any disagreeable duty, always offering himself as a substit-
ute for the "fatigues" of the seminary, such as serving at table.
He seemed to live to help others, and when possible did it
secretly and unobtrusively. I remember setting out on a cold
March day to fish the Hodder river. The snow was on the
ground and a bitter wind swept down the river. I returned at
about five o'clock pm, weary and wet to the skin and, on entering my room, found a warm blazing fire to greet me. Others had
the same experience.'

Much liberty was given in the seminary, but obedience to the
rule was demanded. John Sullivan was faithful to the rule, but in
a way that did not censure others. 'When spoken to in English
during study-time, he tried to answer by sign, but if forced to
speak, it was always in Latin, according to the rule. During my
stay in the seminary I never knew him to transgress that rule or
any other. But what most impressed us was his faith and spirit
of prayer. He was one of the first to morning prayer and the last
to leave the chapel at night visit. At Mass and Communion he

was undemonstrative ... But after receiving Holy Communion he seemed wrapped in prayer ... One felt that here was a man that lived and walked with God.' 'One day I came into the chapel unobserved', Fr Nolan commented, 'and saw him kneeling in his characteristic attitude, slightly bent from his shoulders and hips, his hands barely resting on the bench, the head to one side, with eyes fixed on the tabernacle and the lips moving. For about ten minutes I kept watching him, for it was a lesson to me. I wondered that any man could have such a lively faith, and I recalled what a Dutch scholastic had said some months before, "Mr Sullivan actually talks to Jesus in the chapel".'

On leaving the seminary in September 1904, a year after John Sullivan, Mr Nolan 'went to bid goodbye to the superior, Father Michael Maher, author of the well-known text-book on psychology. I thanked him for his kindness to me and told him how much I owed to the English province. He answered, "The seminary owes something to the Irish province. The Irish province sent us Mr Sullivan. To have a man of God living in our midst is a special mark of God's favour to us".'[71]

Such impressions were confirmed by many others who lived at St Mary's Hall at that time. They told of his kindness to the old priests living in the seminary, to foreign scholastics when they arrived, and his rapport with local farmers whom he met on his walks and by his empathy won their affection. Fr John Turner SJ, who wrote to Fr McGrath about his recollections, spoke of John's 'apartness' but not aloofness. He was 'the most regular of men' but 'was not vexed by the irregularity of others'. Fr Toner recalled John's long sermon in the refectory on St Monica, which made a considerable impression; and that he always tried to hide his ability, never displaying 'his brilliance in classes, responding hesitantly to questions'. 'I can see him', he added, 'hurrying with his head down to the next apostolic labour just as he went about at the seminary.'[72]

One student, who was beginning his third year of philosophy, fell into a deep groove of depression. John Sullivan, who was in his first year, encouraged him to go on walks with him, during which he enlivened the way by stories of famous trials he had witnessed or of which he had heard his father speak, and gradually his companion emerged from the depths. He only realised much later that John had gone on all these walks for his sake. He then made an observation largely borne out by John's life, 'that in whatever surroundings Father Sullivan found himself, he seemed to look around and ask himself, "Is there anybody here who needs help and whom I can help?" Having found such, he gave himself up to them. To get to know Father Sullivan properly you had to be in some sort of need or distress.'[73]

Not all his fellow-students were so impressed. Some, perhaps thinking him too good to be true, refused any assistance from him, brusquely rebuffing any overtures to take over their chores. Mr Sullivan went on his way seemingly unmoved, and on the next occasion came around again to offer his services. Then, and in later life, he seemed to be proof against a snub. His humility, self-detachment, was such that to some it seemed artificial, while John's admirers would say that it seemed artificial only because it was so unusual.[74]

Theology and Ordination

At the end of philosophical studies, most Jesuit scholastics were sent to the Jesuit colleges for three or four years, to teach and involve themselves in school activities. John, presumably because of his age, was not given this experience. In 1904, he was sent straight to Milltown Park, Dublin, for his theology studies. His life there was much as it had been at Stonyhurst, with stories of kindness and thoughtfulness towards fellow students, faithful adherence to the rules, much time spent in prayer and, in addition, though not yet a priest, he paid frequent visits to the patients in the Hospice for the Dying and in the Royal Hospital for Incurables at Donnybrook. In this latter institution, he devoted most time to the men's cancer ward. At his studies, he was a sound rather than an outstanding theologian. As might be expected, he was more at home in canon law and the positive teachings of moral theology than in more metaphysical questions. As always he was very thorough in his preparations, and this was carried through in a special way in his practising of the ceremonies of the Mass.

He was ordained at Milltown Park on Sunday 28 July 1907, by Archbishop Walsh of Dublin. The inscription on his ordination card carried the stock quotation from Psalm 115: '*Quid retribuam Domino pro omnibus quae retribuit mihi?*' – 'What shall I give to the Lord for all that he has given me?' He was to respond to that question with all the generosity of his wholehearted temperament.

Becoming a Catholic in 1896 had marked a change in life and in many of his friends and contacts, but John remained a free man, an independent man of means. Once he took his vows of obedience, chastity and poverty in the Society of Jesus, he put aside his independence and his possessions. He entered on that new way of life with that full commitment, that thoroughness that had marked his studies. This led him along a road of prayer, fasting, and asceticism as his expression of commitment to Jesus Christ. John seemed to believe that his thoroughgoing, all out nature could have led him down a very different road had it not been for the prayers of his mother. His ordination was a seal on his religious commitment. He was to proceed further in his self-giving by increasing his Spartan lifestyle, increasing his selfless work for others, especially the sick poor, devoting more time to prayer, and by a commitment to external poverty in his clothes. He said his first Mass at the convent of the Irish Sisters of Charity, Mount St Anne's, Milltown; and his second at the Carmelite monastery, Firhouse, Tallaght, Co Dublin.

In that year of his ordination, the number of men in the Irish Province was 354: 174 priests, 120 scholastics, and 60 coadjutor brothers. Of these, one hundred served in Australia, working in the colleges and churches founded there by the Irish Jesuits since they undertook the Australian Mission in the 1860s. Immediately after his ordination, Father Sullivan was appointed to the teaching staff at Clongowes Wood College, Co Kildare, where he spent most of the rest of his life. He went there that autumn.

Before he left Milltown Park, however, an incident occurred which was the first of many mysterious occurrences in his life as a priest. He went to visit the Royal Hospital for Incurables, as it was then called, at Donnybrook. It seems to have been shortly after his ordination, for it is recalled that he gave many patients his blessing. He was asked to visit a female patient, who was suffering from lupus in the head, which had begun to affect her mind, and preparations were being made to remove her to a mental hospital. He remained with the patient for a long time praying over her. The next day her mind was completely restored, and remained so until her death; and she was able to restore friendships which she had disrupted as a result of her mental stress.[75]

CHAPTER FOURTEEN

Teacher and Spiritual Father

Clongowes Wood College, to which Father Sullivan was assigned, had been founded in 1814, in the estate and property known as Castle Brown, near Naas, Co Kildare. John's arrival in 1907 brought the membership of the community to thirty-three: 11 priests, 13 scholastics, and 9 brothers.

He was appointed to the teaching staff. He did well with some classes but, in general, was not considered an effective teacher. He avoided severity as a means of keeping order, but he had not the dominant personality that could maintain discipline without the threat of punishment. He was self-effacing, and his speech was hurried and indistinct, and his enthusiasm for his subject sometimes outran the capacity of his class. Despite such shortcomings he was kept on as a teacher and, before long, he was also appointed 'spiritual father' – the priest who looked after the spiritual well-being of the boys and also took an interest in their general happiness and welfare.

There is no shortage of testimony from past students on him as teacher and as spiritual father. Again, a few examples will have to suffice.

Two recollections

The first is from Henry Gerrard, who became an officer in the British army and later a priest in England. He met Fr Sullivan in 1908 at the beginning of his teaching career, before he became spiritual father. He noted what he considered to be the result of his legal training, but in fact was a practice recommended by St Ignatius: 'He recognised in every question two sides, each with merits, but only one could be adopted.' His advice was 'write pros and cons in two columns, and one would surely outweigh the other'. Gerrard referred to Fr Sullivan's 'diffident manner and speech', how 'he could be quite oblivious of his surroundings, whether in private house, class or confessional – the same hurried speech with calculated pauses'. Livy was his favourite author. He enjoyed accounts of 'night attacks, surprises ... a series of short, sharp encounters, which ended most suitably in the punishment of the loser's audacity'. 'Audacious' was a favourite word of his. Gerrard understood that Fr John's father used it frequently. He continued: 'He took First Arts class for both Latin and Apologetics in the year 1909-1910, before he became Spiritual Father. We used to look forward to his classes, to hear still more of his famous "Muratori fragment". He was a student, too, of English politics and referred at times to "the power of the Nonconformists". He had a regard for, and perhaps an acquaintance with Sir Henry Campbell Bannerman.'

His 'Muratori fragment' referred to his interest in the Muratorian fragment (discovered by Ludivico Antonio Muratori) which was a portion of an early Christian document in Latin containing a copy of perhaps the oldest known list of books of the New Testament, and which seemed to date the canon of most New Testament books to the second century.[76] Fr Sullivan's keen interest led to his being known for a while as 'Muratori' or 'Mury'; and the fragment was used as a red herring by pupils not too well prepared to cope with the allotted portion of Livy. Nevertheless, it was recognised that Fr Sullivan was a devoted and hard-working teacher, and he had the reputation of being able to pull even the most backward candidate through his Matriculation examination. One of his main reasons for joining the Jesuits, he told one student, was because so much of their work was devoted to the education of young people. 'He told me that there was no higher calling than teaching and training the youth of the country; that it was a vocation very dear to Almighty God.'[77]

He could be severe enough at times with a real idler, but there was never any harshness in his severity. His most severe reproach was 'You never do a stroke of work', or for an egregious blunder – 'You deserve to be locked up' or 'You should be scourged'.[78] There seems to have been general agreement among numerous past pupils on his sense of humour and his humourous anecdotes, his habit of pushing his hand through his hair, and that he was looked on as 'a saint'.

Again with reference to the years 1908-1912, Rev Eric Fair, DD, professor of Education, University College Galway, remembered hearing during his first year in Clongowes that Fr Sullivan was the son of the Lord Chancellor of Ireland, a position boys associated with 'swank'. But Fr Sullivan although he was 'the essence of gentlemanliness … in his whole bearing, in his gentle courtesy to even the smallest boys, in his simplicity, in his accent, even in his use of the famous word 'audacious', he was the very antithesis of "swank".'[79]

One major witness, and friend of John Sullivan, was another army man, Captain Sidney B. Minch, who had been captain of Clongowes in 1911-12:

> To me he was different in every way from other masters. In his private room I had many hours with him during my last year. He went to great pains helping me to learn *Cataline*, which was the Latin text prescribed for the Senior Grade Intermediate Examination. The disedifying picture of Roman life seemed hurtful to his delicate and sensitive mind … The many visits which I paid him involved a certain amount of suffering for me. I lost my playhour, and in winter I knew I had to face a cold and chilly room. The fire in the room was almost non-existent, as was the little covering on his bed.

'I found Father John at his best on walks during that same last year. With his hat crushed any old way under his arm, he started in a half-run, head well forward, praising everything that nature had to show. How he talked! He found what you were interested in, and then brought God or some saint right into the middle of it so naturally that even our young minds became aware of his constant preoccupation with the things of God.'

Minch's final year coincided with the excitement generated by the passage of the Home Rule Bill under the Liberal government led by Asquith and Campbell Bannerman. Father Sullivan, Minch insisted, was not an isolated, uninformed religious. He spoke of 'the great scientists, statesmen and soldiers of those days' who 'were well known to him, then, with a jump, he was off to ancient Greece or Rome, the Holy Land, then on to Newman, Sir William Butler,[80] and then to St Augustine. Every now and again he would slip aside to visit some poor people living in a humble cottage. We would see him kneeling at the bedside of the invalid. As a matter of fact, he always knelt with us to hear our confession, also.'

'He had a very distinguished face when he really looked at you, but he kept his eyes downwards so much that this seldom appeared. The dried appearance of his cheeks and the semi-parchedness of his lips indicated to us that Father John took very little interest in food or any creature comforts. His hands too were dry, and had a parched feeling. He was fascinated by the heroism of great saints, particularly those who had saved themselves from a life of terrible indulgence. How often do I remember him referring to St Augustine and St Mary Magdalene. He spoke to me of St Paul as "a great fellow, a great fellow". Father John did admire tremendously the real fighter. He took an interest in the games at Clongowes when he was there, and after an out-match he would sympathise or congratulate as the case might be. His expressions were "too bad, too bad, you lost yesterday" or "that's great, you won yesterday". One day he said, "You win nothing unless you know how to lose." It was only in after life that the significance of this came home to me.'

'I knew him even better when I left Clongowes, during the Great War, and afterwards when I fetched him from Rathfarnham to help my father during his last moments on this earth. I remember him well kneeling at the bedside, his socks, which were badly shrunk, just slightly above his boots – you could actually see his shins. Before he left I realised for the first time how happy an event death could be. In the same old clothes he always wore, he assisted at my marriage and disappeared immediately it was over.

'When I visited him at Rathfarnham he complained of his appointment as rector, in 1919, which he could not account for. I asked him laughingly if he was afraid, and I shall never forget his distant look when he replied: "When I was told that I was to be rector I had been for some time meditating on the humility of Our Lord in the stable at Bethlehem and this doesn't seem to me to fit in properly".'

Sidney Minch concluded:

> As I have said at the outset, his memory is vividly before me. I had a tremendous affection for him, and I know how easy it would be to exaggerate in writing about him, and how much he would hate it. I have, therefore, purposely kept accurately to what I remember of him.
>
> There is one thought which today I still carry with me, and which he alone gave me. It is this. 'You'll never have to fight alone in this world, although we leave Our Divine Saviour to fight alone constantly.'[81]

George Little Remembers

As Sidney Minch completed his final year at Clongowes, another boy entered the school who was to have vivid recollections of John Sullivan. On the centenary of John Sullivan's birth in 1961, he still remembered him in detailed clarity, the memory standing out like a Rembrandt etching. George Little, who became a well-known Dublin physician and a writer on Irish history and archaeology, entered Clongowes in 1911, and for two years Fr Sullivan taught him junior Latin.

'He stood some five feet ten in height. I have heard an unobservant person say that Father Sullivan dressed like a tramp – this was far from the fact. His clothes were green from age, the elbows of his coat and knees of his trousers darned obviously by himself; his boots shapeless from age and patched, but carefully blackened; his clothes as carefully brushed – in short a signifi-cant picture of a gentleman in old clothes. But to think of how he was dressed was always an afterthought. It was the man himself who held all one's attention.

'His features were long but well-proportioned; a face classi-cal in cast, serious from absorption with a purpose and the struggle to accomplish that purpose. Besides the lines of concen-tration on his forehead, at his eyes and from nostrils to his mouth corners, his skin was covered by a fine mesh of wrinkles giving it something of the appearance of old, cream kid-leather; his hands similarly dry and wrinkled.

'Father Sullivan's hair was reddish brown – dry, with no ten-dency to lie flat; his eyebrows were thick above his deep-set, usually downcast eyes. I am now satisfied that the condition I have described of skin and hair resulted from avitiminosis [the lack or one or more minerals], caused probably by the diet he had imposed on himself in self-denial. His eyes were usually cast down, but when he strove to understand you or to emphas-ise some point, they looked straight into yours ... Having made his point, he dropped them again.

'It is generally said that Father Sullivan was an ineffective teacher. I may not judge this opinion, but I can recall that in my class so interesting did he make Caesar's story that several of the twelve-year-old boys finished the text before it had been half construed by him. No small achievement for any teacher to imbue his pupils with such interest. I can still remember his dry chuckle at the bald statement, *Orgetorix mortuus est.* 'Yes boys', he said, 'the poor king undoubtedly died. But note how well Caesar's economy of words served both his own interests and the truth.' Such little turns of donnish humour were fairly fre-quent with him, and never failed to delight us.

'He was also a "sport" in class. This word in a schoolboy's vocabulary means that he never took advantage of a situation in class, always befriending a boy even when he was obviously blameworthy.' George Little gave an example from his own ex-perience. He had played an unkind trick on another pupil. Fr

Sullivan observing it, declared: 'A most audacious fellow, Little. Kneel down there', pointing to a spot near the blackboard. Little's concern was that the very efficient prefect of studies, Fr James Daly, who had a reputation for severity, might come into the classroom and see him. Suddenly he heard a jingle of keys in the gallery outside, and grabbing the duster he stood up and began cleaning the blackboard. Fr Daly's eagle eye swept the room, then he bowed to Fr Sullivan and left. 'With a smile around the corners of his rigid lips', Fr Sullivan turned to Little, 'Most audacious fellow! Go back to your place. Use the wit God gave you for useful things.' 'Gratefully ashamed', Little explained, 'I returned to my place, while he rewrote what had been rubbed out.'

'The recollection of this story makes me understand now why it was that Father Sullivan had no difficulty at all in keeping order in his class. We would have been ashamed to trouble him. By little ways, by little things – for no one ever told us – we were confirmed in our belief that this man was a man of God. Perhaps he was the only person we would know to whom we could ever apply in utter conviction the description "saint".' 'I think he liked our class. He had no great regard for the merely successful. I think I learned first from him that the measure of a man is what he does with what he has got.'

The memory of a walk to Maynooth in 1912 stood out in George Little's memory. 'It was on a holiday – or playday, as we called our rare freedoms – that the walk took place. Some twenty of us started with him and we soon found that his extraordinary trot was quite tireless, and most difficult for our short legs to keep up with. But on we tore, until at last someone timidly asked where we were heading for. 'We have only time for a short walk', he said, 'We'll go to Maynooth.' Maynooth! Eight long miles away! But we had our pride, so made no protest. On the way we talked away to him about our many interests, and the time and the miles passed quickly. On our arrival, though, our leader, looking at the great clock in the college quadrangle, was much taken aback. It was late, so 'No time to sit down, boys, no time at all. We must return to Clongowes at once.'

They made a show of spirit in their talk on the way back. 'Soon, however, the miles beat us to silence. Then Father Sullivan, pitying our fatigue, began to talk. In his quick, earnest speech he told us of Greece, great in art, greater in virtue … Yes, he had seen that fatal valley of Thermopylae. As his speech ran on, we could see the Persian hosts gathering on the hills and filing down the secret pass which treachery had opened for them against the Spartans. And the leader, Leonidas, appraised the situation: the doom their honour demanded of them all, he recognised with the certainty of the professional soldier. And his men, understanding him, saw to their arms. They then (like the ancient Irish before a battle) fell to singing and combing their long hair … The rapid earnest voice ran on. We could hear the bronze-clad Persians thunder down the crags to die on the Spartan swords. Sword on shield, groans and cries of men fighting, echoed down the years. Then it was all over. In resounding Greek he declaimed Simonides' epitaph over the fallen. Translated it runs:

> Go, chance pilgrim, tell the Spartans that in this place,
> obedient to their laws, we died.

'He was silent a little, then whispered, more to himself than to us, something about 'the beauty of order' and 'the splendour of obedience'.

'We were very tired when we reached Clongowes, but I think we all felt that something had a little ennobled our fatigue.'

Dr Little concluded his imaginatively evocative tribute with a visit to St Francis Xavier Church, Gardiner Street, Dublin, 'to view the stately sarcophagus in which now rest the remains of the old soldier of Christ'.[82]

A Characteristic Letter

Around the period referred to by George Little, Fr Sullivan wrote a characteristic letter to a boy who had just left Clongowes and was considering his future in a retreat at Milltown Park, Dublin. The boy, who bore the historic name of Daniel O'Connell, preserved the letter as a cherished possession. On 1 September 1913, Fr John Sullivan addressed the young man by his surname, a practice very common then, and not at all formal.

> My dear O'Connell,
> I write a few lines to say that I hope to remember all your intentions at Mass during your retreat. I hope and pray that our dear Lord will give you grace and light clearly to see His holy will and the Strength and courage to carry it out.

[Fr Sullivan then quoted from a letter which he had received from another old Clongownian saying how happy he was in the noviciate] He continued:

> For myself I can only say with St Augustine, 'Too late have I known Thee, too late have I loved Thee, O beauty ever ancient and ever new! Too late have I known Thee!'
> If you only knew all the misery, sin, sorrow and suffering there is in this world, and how much a priest can do to comfort, console and raise the fallen, you would not hesitate to decide. If you could hear the voices of countless souls crying to you: 'Come over and help us'!
> Kindly forgive these hurried few lines and believe me always,
> Yours Affectionately in Christ,
> John Sullivan SJ

The last sentence seems to echo, consciously or unconsciously, the passage in the *Confession* of St Patrick in which he recounts how he heard, in a dream, voices from 'near the Western Sea' calling him back to Ireland.

The recipient of the letter became clear about his vocation during the retreat, joined the Jesuits, and, after distinguished scientific studies, became director of the observatory at Riverview College, Sydney, Australia, and then director of the Papal Observatory at Castel Gandolfo and president of the Pontifical Academy of Sciences.[83]

As it was in the beginning

Years later, in Fr Sullivan's final years, the impressions remained the same. Roland Burke Savage, a bright, rather academic youth, commenced in Clongowes in 1926. Fr Sullivan recognised the young boy's need. 'From my first few days in the house', Burke Savage recalled, 'he began to invite me up to his room from time to time, where he would talk of people we knew or of books. Strangely enough … he always made me feel as if I were talking to an equal with whom I was on the friendliest terms.' Fr Sullivan's room became a haven from some of the pressures of boarding school life. Speaking of books, 'the main topics of conversation were the Latin and Greek classics. Often he would read off a translation of Homer, or Aeschylus, or John Chrysostom. Horace or St Augustine were his favourite Latin authors.' 'Only a quarter of his conversation was strictly on spiritual topics.'

It was Roland's impression that Fr Sullivan did not 'really understand all the difficulties of growing boys', especially their adolescent struggle with sexuality. 'He gave the impression that grace had made the path of holiness much easier for him than for most.' Roland did not go to Fr Sullivan for confession, but many of the so-called 'toughs' did. 'He was very understanding of disappointments, upsets, homesickness, or mere loneliness' and seemed almost able to sense their presence. Without any mention of them, he would begin to talk of the 4th Station of the Cross or some other scene in the Passion and, as a result, your own small sorrow would be lost in the larger one'.[84] He had a special devotion to the Stations of the Cross and tended to give prayer at certain stations as a penance at confession.

Fr Sullivan gave short talks to the whole school, instead of evening rosary, from time to time. In Burke Savage's view, they were 'very effective'. 'Despite his little mannerisms, the refrains of "an all that" and "out in the world there", the obvious sincerity, directness and optimism of his talks impressed me very much at the time … Love of Christ and of Our Lady seemed to be the topics that came easiest to him.'[85]

A Somewhat Different View. Michael Sweetman's Recollections
Twenty-five years after Fr Sullivan's death, Fr Michael Sweetman, later to be celebrated for his own courageous commitment to the poor, offered his distinctive memories and assessment in the *Clongownian*. He had been a boy in Clongowes, from 1925 to 1931, and was one of those, in his early years, who made Fr Sullivan's life difficult. Fr John had Michael's class for history. Their lack of cooperation extended even to setting a fire in one of the covered desks, and shouting 'Fire' when smoke came through the inkwell-hole. 'Were we sorry?' Sweetman asked. 'I think we were a little ashamed at heart, but it didn't show in that early adolescent stage of the struggle to avoid education.'

'Even after his earnest and moving sermons the boys would imitate him, not unkindly, running their fingernails through the hair just over the ear as Father Sullivan did, and adding 'There' to every sentence of a description of some poor woman dying gruesomely of cancer.' Fr Sullivan spoke frequently in his sermons of the suffering of the sick he tended, asking prayers for them, and of the wider suffering in the world. 'As they watched him swiftly hobbling along the galleries from one chapel to another', the boys' only comment would probably have been 'There goes Johnny O.' 'He was called this, affectionately and irreverently (from a frequent misconception that his name was O'Sullivan). The boys themselves never called him anything else. He was taken entirely for granted: there happened to be a saint in the place, and what more natural.'

'He was, at the time I am writing of, in the last stages of sanctity: the turns and falls and halts were over; he was in the final straight.' But he was no closer to really understanding boys. 'His attempts at direct personal contact were sometimes fantastically unsuited to attract a boy. I had the privilege of being invited to come up to his room and translate with him the *Choral Odes* of Aristophanes – "The most beautiful things in all literature, there …" The strange thing is that in the last year in school an invitation to come up and talk about God or vocation would not have been at all unwelcome. He didn't, naturally, understand boys.'

Michael, in fact, in his final years at school often walked and talked with Fr Sullivan, and all his life he cherished the memory. 'Perhaps the most valuable experience in knowing Father Sullivan was the opportunity constantly to observe a man who peered out uneasily at the world of the senses, who had obvious trouble in bringing his mind to bear on other than spiritual reali- ties ... Another thing – and how peculiar was its combining with the first we only realised much later – was, that he would do anything for you, absolutely anything. There was no limit im- posed willingly by him; you felt that you could make any de- mands on him and they would never be refused by him from mere disinclination or on account of the cost to himself. In plain words, he loved you. It was with that strange unsentimental emotion called "supernatural charity", but in him it was sincere and trustworthy.'

Fr Sullivan, Sweetman concluded, was 'meek and fearless' and was 'an absolutely honest man'. There was no sham. 'He in- spired us with belief in the value of a life lived for God and for God's weak and suffering children ... As boys we took it for granted that this patient, clear-eyed, old priest, with the dry wrinkled hands and furrowed face, lived wholly for God; only later did we become aware that that was a very unusual thing to do.'[86]

CHAPTER FIFTEEN

Asceticism and Prayer, and serving the Sick

Fr Sullivan's asceticism was widely known. Servants spoke of his bed being untouched and expressed the belief that he slept on the floor, and they claimed to have found stones in his boots. As if to give some credence to this last, when brought to Vincent's Hospital with his final illness his feet were found to be in a severely damaged condition. Frequently, he slept only for a couple of hours, praying until late in the chapel, and rising very early in the morning. He gave retreats in many convents where, almost invariably, the hospitality was proverbial, but the greatest culinary efforts made little impression. He took only two meals at the convent of Mercy, Skibbereen, Co Cork. They consisted of 'a very moderate breakfast and rice and milk for dinner'; while, at the Carmelite Convent, Rathmines, Dublin, 'his diet was a little boiled rice with a little milk and dry bread for dinner and in the evening bread and tea'. When at the Mercy Convent, Baggott Street, Dublin, the sister in charge of meals remonstrated: 'But, Father, you'll never be able to keep yourself up on that', he replied significantly, 'That's just it; I want to keep myself down.'[87]

Not surprisingly, after returning to Clongowes from Rathfarnham in 1924, he began to suffer much from stomach trouble. This prevented him sleeping. His superiors ordered him to consult the college doctor, who told him he must eat more or he would die. As a result, he began to take a boiled egg, bread and butter, as well as porridge, and added a small dish of rice to potatoes and bread at dinner.

At Prayer
Again and again, fellow Jesuits, pupils, people where he gave

retreats, told of Fr John's intensity in praying the Stations of the Cross. He seemed to enter personally into the sufferings of Jesus. Frequently, too, people had come across him kneeling or lying in the darkness of a chapel. Sometimes his prayer was accompanied by loud, wordless groans. Fr James Tomkin recalled how one night, at about 10.30, he was in a corner of a chapel in Clongowes and he heard a side-door open and someone come in, go on his knees a short way up the aisle, and begin to pray and groan audibly. He knew it was Father Sullivan. He had never heard anyone praying as he did. 'The whole man, body and spirit, was in the prayer. He uttered no distinct words ... After a considerable time he arose, came up midway between the door and the altar rails, went on his knees again and continued his prayer and groaning in spirit more intensely. Then he rose again, came up and went on his knees a short distance from the altar rails. Another long interval and he stood up, opened the gates of the sanctuary, came in a few paces, and knelt down before the tabernacle.' Here again, and more earnestly, he poured forth his prayer and groans. It was about midnight when he finished his prayer. The whole experience reminded Fr Tomkin of St Paul's words in his letter to the Romans, 8:22: 'Ourselves also, who have the first-fruits of the Spirit ... groan within ourselves, waiting for the adoption of the sons of God, the redemption of our body.'

Fr Tomkin at other times had seen Fr Sullivan in quiet prayer in a silent church. He was also impressed by Fr Sullivan's monthly exhortations to the community, which was part of his role as spiritual father to the community. 'He always held the crucifix in his hand when addressing us. He had a great knowledge of the scriptures and a marvellous facility in quoting both scriptures and the (church) Fathers at great length and to the point. He must have had a prodigious memory to quote them so accurately, but it was his mere presence, the crucifix in his hands, the earnestness and fervour of his spirit that gave to his exhortations such a lasting effect.'[88]

Something similar was experienced by the Cistercian Fathers

at their abbey in Roscrea when he gave them a retreat in 1925. Father Columban observed that 'he seemed to just meditate aloud, speaking to his crucifix, rather than to address his listeners … He spoke in simple short sentences with a directness that reached both mind and heart. Father Sullivan seemed wholly absorbed in God, and yet I found him very affable when I approached him for confession and spiritual advice and have ever since remembered his parting words, "Brother, you have a wonderful vocation. Always serve the Lord in great joy".'

Father Oliver observed that the aggregate impression of the retreat was 'that one felt virtue going out from the Father Director, although every natural reason therefore was utterly and palpably lacking. Father Sullivan's appearance was abject' and 'to this day his voice still echoes in my ears. It was raucous and absolutely devoid of intonation, but his very words come back to me precisely because they were so unadorned, so poor in phrase … The text is unadorned. He made it uncouth. "There was Peter there" – such were his reiterated parable-pictures.' 'And yet while directors have come since who brought to God's word every human elegance and grace, it is … a testimony of fact, that of nearly all, I, at any rate, have forgotten both features and phrases. It is my conviction that only the most intense union with God, the almost complete absorption of the human and natural element could account for Father Sullivan's power.'

Friend of the Sick and Needy
Apart from his work as teacher, spiritual father, and retreat director, Father Sullivan was a familiar figure amongst the sick and the needy for miles around Clongowes. He visited them on foot or on an old bicycle. And in time there was an ever-widening circle of others, whom he visited in hospitals and consoled by letter, or who came to him from almost every county in Ireland to ask the intercession of his prayers in their illness and misfortunes. He constantly heard confessions in the People's Church attached to Clongowes Wood College. He had no office for interviewing people who sought his prayers and blessing.

He met them in the porch of the church, and continued before the altar or in the confessional and ended at the font, for he had a great devotion to holy water. People came by bicycle, by horse or ass and cart, or arranged a lift for a sick person in an ancient Ford or a hired car. In later years it was a common sight to see several cars waiting outside the door, in which invalids had been brought to get his blessing. Whatever about the numerous cures and other favours attributed to his prayers, there is no doubt that remarkable trust in the power of his intercession was manifested not only amongst the people in the vicinity of Clongowes, but also in many counties of Ireland.[89]

If someone was sick or in trouble and could not make the journey to Clongowes, he came to them as soon as he heard of their need. Distances did not seem to be a major obstacle. Once he walked fourteen miles there and fourteen miles back to pray with and to bless a sick person. His bicycle brought him on longer journeys, including visits to Dublin and back. One re-markable recorded case concerned a religious sister who had a very serious accident which led to an amputation and then a fur-ther amputation. By letter he learned that she was in a grave condition, fever and delirium had set in. The letter asked his prayers and that he might visit her if he was in Dublin. The post arrived at the school during the morning break. The hospital where the sister lay was over twenty miles from Clongowes. He set out on his bike and arrived in the early afternoon. He went to the patient's room, knelt down, without support, and gave him-self to prayer. After a long time, the nun's restless tossing be-came quiet, and the delirium ceased. She appeared to sleep. Fr Sullivan quietly returned to his bicycle and was back in Clongowes in time for a meeting of the Sodality of Our Lady that evening.[90]

Mathias Bodkin, in his *Port of Tears*, wrote graphically of Fr Sullivan's commitment to people in the vicinity of Clongowes. 'He would answer to any cry of distress … and would keep com-ing day after day and week after week if the pain was great or unyielding or the illness mortal. Or you could command his presence if you were poor enough to need the little gifts of tea, sugar, and food or clothes he allowed himself to receive and pass on.' He was a welcome and frequent caller if someone was struggling to rear a family or endeavouring to bear up under domestic persecution or loss. But as soon as he was no longer needed, he disappeared. 'He would arrive on the old bicycle, riding doggedly down rutted boreens or over wind-swept bog roads; or if you lived closer he might come on foot. You'd see his figure perhaps a good way off, the rather long full coat, the patched boots, the soft hat more often clutched than worn, the beads in one hand and the unmistakable rapid step, almost a trot, that seemed to drive him forward. A quick greeting, then an inquiry, and he'd go straight into the sick room. There'd be a blessing with lavish holy water, and then he'd be down on his knees and praying.' He prayed alone for some time, and then 'the bystanders, and often the sick person, would be asked to join in the rosary or simple ejaculations'. If there was a matter of confession, or other matters of a private nature, the bystanders were asked to leave, and then, on a given signal, they returned to join in the prayers, prayers usually of trust and thanksgiving.

It was generally accepted that Father Sullivan was so close to God that God worked healings of body and spirit through him. 'It is the universality of this impression, the number of stories, which is really impressive. The record of one of them, or even of a number of them, cannot carry the conviction that comes after hearing scores of simple folk, each one quite separate from the rest, tell their own tale, sometimes in almost identical words.'[91] Numerous instances of cures through the intercession of Fr John Sullivan, including cases where doctors gave no hope of recovery, may be read in Fr Fergal McGrath's standard biography, *Father John Sullivan, S.J.*

Prescience

Almost equally remarkable were the instances of Fr Sullivan's prescience. He was sent for in the case of a young man, named Peter, who was taken badly ill. His young wife was expecting a child. Fr Sullivan knelt beside the sick man's bed and prayed. He got the others to join in for an hour and twenty minutes. Then rising from his knees, he said to the wife, in the presence of others, that her husband was going to die. 'He is safe. He will be in heaven before I am half-way to the college.' In fact, he was gone perhaps a quarter of a mile when Peter 'passed away without recovering consciousness or a word or a sigh'. A similar incident is related by the daughter of another family situated near Clongowes that Fr Sullivan visited frequently. Her father was old and had been ailing for some time, but seemed in no immediate danger. There was no change in his condition when Fr Sullivan called unexpectedly. He surprised the household when he asked the man to accompany him to an upstairs room, presumably for confession. They were taken aback to hear the priest say to him unequivocally, 'My good man, you will be with God tonight.' He died peacefully within twenty-four hours.[92]

Such prescience was not confined to matters of life and death: sometimes he would assure a person that employment would be made available, or that domestic circumstances would improve. When rector of Rathfarnham Castle he used to visit fairly frequently the Carmelite convent in the vicinity. The couple who lived in the lodge at the convent gate were used to seeing him pass, but found him rather 'distant'. One day, however, he got off his bicycle and said to the woman without preamble: 'You are in great trouble, but don't worry about it. You have no cause for anxiety.' With that he remounted and rode on. Narrating the incident, the woman explained: 'My husband and I were in fact at the time very much concerned at an unpleasant prospect that threatened us with ruin, but of which we were sure no one but ourselves had any inkling. In fact the threatened trouble never came to anything and we had nothing more to fear.'[93]

Fr Sullivan's years in Clongowes did not happen in a social and political vacuum, and all his time was not taken up by prayer and the care of youth and the sick poor.

The Historical Context

His early years in the college were historic ones for both college and country. In 1912 the union day carried a note of special celebration in the light of the apparent attainment of Home Rule under the leadership of a past student, John Redmond. The pupils' gold medals that year were won by Fergal McGrath and John C. McQuaid, future Archbishop of Dublin, both of whom revered Father Sullivan and were to play a major part in making his life known. In 1914 the centenary celebrations of the college saw college and grounds *en fête* for four days, as convoys of open cars brought hundreds of past students and their spouses from Sallins station where they arrived by special train. Many others, including the chief dignitaries, came down the long festooned avenue in motor cars. The occasion was marked by messages from the Pope and the Jesuit General, by High Mass celebrated by Michael Cardinal Logue, by eloquent addresses from various luminaries, including John Redmond MP, still seen as the future leader of a Home Rule Ireland, and by the presence of numerous personages well-known to John Sullivan – including Chief Baron Christopher Palles, Judge Thomas Bodkin, and the Right Honorable Charles A. O'Connor, Master of the Rolls.[94] For all his shyness and recollectedness, Fr Sullivan made a special effort to chat with and welcome people who visited Clongowes. In Peter Costello's *History of Clongowes Wood College 1814-1989*, there is an interesting photograph of groups of people chatting on Union Day 1910, while the British Army band plays in the background. In one small group, Father Sullivan is to be seen talking animatedly. At times, indeed, he was known to show people around the college and the grounds. He rather gleefully told the story of showing two elderly ladies around, and how at the end, perceiving no doubt his patched clothes and boots, they gave him a half-crown for his trouble. He contributed it to his fund for the deserving poor.

A little over two months after the centenary celebrations, the First World War broke out. By June 1915, some 321 past students had joined up. By the end of the war, according to the

Clongownian of 1919, some 604 had served, of whom 94 had been killed in action or had succumbed to their wounds. All these provided occasions of prayer for Fr Sullivan, as did the many young men who served in the war from the areas around Clongowes and, also, the sons of friends from Portora, Trinity, and his years as barrister.

Meantime, there had been an unpopular revolution in Dublin in 1916 which, largely thanks to the government's over-reaction and reprisals, led to a country-wide rejection of John Redmond's Parliamentary Party and growing public support for Sinn Féin. By 1918 the college felt the effects of the strong anti-government feeling in the country in the wake of the government's foiled plans to introduce conscription.

The Strike by the Staff

There had been plans that winter to hold a concert in the college for wounded soldiers. The servants protested at this, and the rector suspected that if there was a demonstration some of the more nationalist-minded schoolboys would side with the staff. He gave way. The concert did not take place. This was later felt to have been taken by the staff as a sign of weakness on the part of Fr Nicholas Tomkin.[95]

At this time, the Irish Transport and General Workers' Union was rapidly enlarging its membership outside Dublin. It was the union of James Larkin, James Connolly, and Bill O'Brien, and was associated in the minds of many employers with some form of social revolution prompted by socialist agitators. Meetings were held in Co Kildare, and some of the college staff attended one in Clane. Probably inspired by the ITGWU, though not organised by the union, members of the staff, at 7.00 pm on 23 February, handed an ultimatum to the Fr Minister, Fr Potter, who was in charge of the staff and of running of the house. He was to reply to their demands for an increase in wages by 7.15, or else they would withdraw their labour the next day. In fact, they stopped work that very evening, and they were formally dismissed by the minister.

Where did Fr Sullivan feature in all this? He was on good terms with members of staff and had responded to the needs of some of their families. Was his legal advice sought by the minister or rector? The answer is not known. But he almost certainly joined other members of the community in serving the boys' supper that evening, only ten minutes later than usual. The boys were amused, but fourteen of the older boys led by the school captain, Patrick Fleury, volunteered to help with the washing-up and with the preparations for breakfast that had to be made that night. Next day the staff turned up for their own breakfasts, and stayed on the premises all day, but the rector and minister stood firm, feeling they had the law on their side. A message for help was sent to the provincial. The staff left the next day. Four Jesuit brothers arrived from Tullabeg to relieve the situation, and the next day again local help was offered and the community's serving in the boys' refectory came to an end. On 27 February new staff began to arrive. The crisis was over, but the day the staff went on strike passed into the college's folklore.

It raised the question, whether it was right to dismiss all the staff rather than negotiate. Most of the community seemed dismayed at the demand for an increase of wages at a time when prices were falling; and in the background was a fear of social revolution. On the other hand, some Jesuits in the province were outraged by the decision. To Fr Jack Boyd-Barrett, 'who had tried to make the boys aware of the social injustices in Irish society, ... the affair seemed to express the *de haut en bas* attitude of many Jesuits'.[96]

Once again, there is no information on Fr Sullivan's views. His compassion for the families of the dismissed workers may be assumed, as also his continued focus, through all eventualities, on a life of prayer, self-denial, and the practical service of others.

In July 1919, to his surprise and discomfort, it was announced that he was to move from Clongowes to become rector of the house of studies at Rathfarnham Castle, Dublin.

CHAPTER SIXTEEN

Rector of Rathfarnham Castle

Rathfarnham Castle was built in the sixteenth century by Adam Loftus, Church of Ireland Archbishop of Armagh and then of Dublin. It passed through many hands before being bought by the Irish Jesuits in 1913 as a residence and house of studies for their university students. The community at Rathfarnham Castle in 1919 was composed of ten priests, some working in the castle, others giving missions or retreats throughout the country; two Jesuit brothers, engaged in the house and in the grounds; and fourteen scholastics who were students at University College Dublin. These, during Fr Sullivan's first year, were a particularly able group of young men, whom novelist Kate O'Brien remembered as the 'very well-controlled and holy young men out of Rathfarnham Castle'.[97] They included, Edward Coyne, a future professor of theology and president of the Irish Cooperative Agricultural Agency, Mathias Bodkin, author, missioner, military chaplain, Thomas Fleming, a future professor of theology and philosophy, Arthur Little, future professor of philosophy and poet, Daniel O'Connell, future scientist and head of the Vatican Observatory, and other men destined to play prominent parts in the work of the Irish Jesuit Province and its foreign missions: Maurice Dowling, in Africa, John O'Meara, as administrator and professor in Hong Kong and Canton, and at home – Tim Mulcahy, Hugh O'Neill, Paul O'Flanagan, Leonard Gallagher, and Joseph O'Connor.

For the first three years, Fr Sullivan, in addition to being overall rector, was prefect of studies for these students and their successors. Not an easy task at any time, but carrying added tension in those years when the Irish political struggle took on the semblance of open warfare and government forces outraged public opinion by their acts of intimidation and violence. And in subsequent years there was the added problem presented by the Civil War, when members of the same family turned against each other and when it was a major challenge to preserve unity and charity amongst a diverse body of young men. It would appear that John Sullivan's kindness, goodness, and other-worldliness had such a salutary effect that there was no expression of the explosive feelings likely to have been present below the surface.

Various impressions

One of the students in Fr Sullivan's first year, Maurice Dowling, later observed that the rector 'furthered the sanctity and spirit of each of the scholastics in a marked degree and, by extreme prudence and charity and very good judgement, he preserved the vocation of several which might otherwise have been lost'. He adapted to the academic difficulties experienced by the students at University College Dublin by providing 'special facilities regarding meals for the students with late lectures' and 'he allowed students into the evening debates of various university societies'.[98] Dowling found him very approachable and relished his quick sense of humour. On one occasion, on entering Fr Sullivan's room, he saw the bed covered with cakes, oranges, sweets, and bottles of lemonade. Rather daringly for a student, he remarked: 'Some people do themselves well.' 'Ah yes', replied the rector in similar vein, 'I have to look after myself.' It was known that the delicacies were for an old priest who had had a mental breakdown. Another incident recalled by Dowling, was when he received permission from Fr Sullivan to visit an aunt who had been badly shaken in an accident. Because of difficulties in travel and the tramway timetable, he arrived so late at her house that it was a question of returning at once or returning at a very late hour. He chose the second alternative, and on the following day he was summoned to the rector's room to explain the irregularity. Deciding to take the initiative, he opened, 'Father, may I state my case?' 'You know you have no case.' The young man persisted. 'My case is that I was late out of obedience. You gave me leave to visit my aunt. I presumed, therefore, that you wanted me to see her. So, in being late, I was fulfilling your orders.' Fr Sullivan looked at him and began to laugh. 'Get out, get out, get out', he exclaimed.[99]

Not all were as favourably disposed as Maurice Dowling. His contemporary, Joseph G. O'Connor, claimed that Fr Sullivan did not seem to appreciate their academic difficulties. 'He was not the most suitable person to have in charge of young religious, because he entered religion later in life and had not himself the experience of being a young religious.' Father O'Connor admitted, however, that the rector was 'very approachable and easy to deal with'.[100]

A mixture of the rector's humour and realism was encapsulated in the experience of Daniel O'Connell as a scholastic. Entering the rector's room, he saw to his amazement on the bed a bottle of whiskey and a bottle of wine. Fr Sullivan, who had had him as a pupil in Clongowes, assured him: 'It's all right. I'm not going on the booze. Those are for a poor old woman. They do more to keep her heart up than I can.'[101] He was very conscious of the evil caused to homes by the excessive consumption of alcohol, but he was far from a legalist.

Fr Joseph O'Connor was not the only one to feel that Fr Sullivan failed to understand the difficulties his students faced in endeavouring to take part in university life while at the same time observing the reasonable restraints of religious discipline.[102] The rector, in Father Bodkin's recollection, was inclined to exaggerate the difficulties that could arise from the co-education of young religious men and women, but he 'referred all such matters to Fr Provincial (T.V. Nolan) and appeared to acquiesce in the latter's broadminded treatment of them'.[103] Fr Sullivan could be amused, however, by students' misreading of his views in this respect. Discussing with one of his students about his classical studies at the university, he asked: 'Are there any ladies in your class?' The student replied that there were two. 'What are they like?' 'Rather plain', the student responded.

With a gleam of amusement, the rector exclaimed: 'In God's name, there, I didn't mean that. What are they like in Latin?'[104]

It was also remarked that Fr Sullivan had not sufficient confidence in himself to make prompt decisions; yet when serious difficulties arose he was very calm and, being detached from personal feeling, was able to take an objective view of the failings of his subjects.[105] His calmness, empathy, and detached judgement were particularly called for in 1919-1920. His scholastics attending University College were exposed to the college's strong nationalist spirit, and some of them had friends, maybe relatives, involved in the Troubles. Feeling was at a high intensity in October 1920 as Terence McSwiney's long hunger-strike drew to an end. Under the date, 29 October 1920, *The Belvederian* reflected public feeling: 'No school today. We are in mourning for the great Lord Mayor of Cork whose spirit the greatest of the Empires could not enslave.' And very shortly afterwards there was further mourning on the hanging of the former Belvedere pupil and the current student of UCD, Kevin Barry, which brought feeling to fever pitch at University College and evoked from *The Belvederian* the searing comment: 'Our school-fellow scarcely a year ago … meets a criminal's end at the hands of the freer of small nations.' And to add to the tensions of the time, Rathfarnham Castle was raided by the Black and Tans, the most undisciplined section of the security forces.

Fr John's diffidence about himself meant that he did not take an active part in directing the studies of his young men, but on occasion he provided coaching for the weaker students. Very occasionally he attended a paper of one of the students at the university. As noted earlier, the embarrassment of the student gave way to surprise when he saw the welcome accorded his rector by senior academics, who were well aware of his distinguished university reputation. Embarrassment at the clothes of Fr Sullivan was accentuated, at times, by his complete absence of human respect. Travelling by train or bus alongside one of the scholastics, the rector quietly said the rosary, holding the beads in his hat on his knee.

The young Jesuits, nevertheless, like others in the community, were impressed by their rector's homilies, and especially by their depth of spirituality, the long quotations from scripture and the Fathers without reference to a note, the application of the material to their own spiritual needs and to the importance of hard work. Throughout, he held a crucifix in his hands and kept his eyes on it. Some felt that because of his own high standards, he expected too much of them. He countered the emphasis on hard work, however, by urging students individually not to work too hard.

As rector, Fr John undertook greater abstemiousness with respect to food, while maintaining his commitment to the care of the sick in so far as his other duties permitted. He also continued to give retreats and instructions to members of various religious communities, and took a special interest in St Mary's open-air hospital for children at Cappagh, near Dublin, then in its early stages. Many doubted its establishment in the Irish climate, but Fr Sullivan was one of those who were confident it would succeed. He was invited to bless the foundation stone of the first large extension in 1923, and he became 'a familiar figure at the hospital, hurrying up the avenue, giving the children a blessing as he passed, inquiring about the progress of the work, and invariably departing without accepting the slightest refreshment'.[106]

His interest in the welfare of the poor and his social conscience led to his strong support for the workmen's retreats, for which a retreat house was built at Rathfarnham in 1922, and for the work of the Legion of Mary.

Workmen's Retreats. Frank Duff and the Legion
The workmen's retreats, in 1921-22, were in the hands of the redoubtable Fr Richard Devane, who had been a diocesan priest in Limerick and, as a Jesuit, became noted for his care of young offenders and was termed 'the Father of unmarried mothers' because of his public defence of their rights. Late in life, he became well known as an author. He experienced constant encourage-

Sir Edward Sullivan, Lord Chancellor of Ireland.

Lady Elizabeth Sullivan (née Bailey).

The Sullivan children about 1866.
Front, from left, Edward, John, William;
back, Robert and Annie.

John Sullivan, aged sixteen, in 1877.

John Sullivan as a young man: 'The best dressed man in Dublin.'

Union Day 1910 at Clongowes.
On the right, Fr Sullivan talks animatedly to past students.

Fr Sullivan's room in Clongowes.

Clongowes College as it was in John's time.

Inside the People's Church at Clongowes,
where Fr John prayed, heard confessions, and met people.

Arrival of the remains at Gardiner Street, 1960,
being received by Archbishop McQuaid.

Praying at the shrine shortly after the remains were placed there.
A constant stream of people come there to pray.

The best known picture of Fr John Sullivan, taken in his later years.

The Rt Hon W. E. Gladstone, Prime Minister of Great Britain
on four occasions between 1868 and 1894.
Below: Judge James Murphy,
friend and adviser of the young John Sullivan.

St George's Church of Ireland Church, near Eccles St.,
where John was baptised.

Portora Royal School, Enniskillen, where John spent six happy years.

Trinity College, Dublin, attended by John Sullivan, 1879-1885.

Glencairn, home of Judge Murphy and his family,
where John was always welcome.

Professor John P. Mahaffy, TCD

Cork Street Convent and Night Shelter.

Rathfarnham Castle, with the Retreat House to the right.

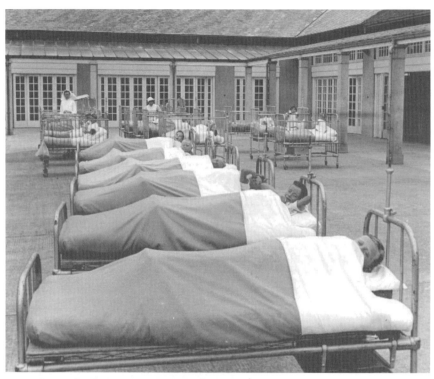

Cappagh Children's Hospital, where Fr Sullivan was a frequent visitor, and a strong supporter of the management and staff.

ment from Fr Sullivan who, for all his poverty in relation to himself, was prepared to spare no expense where the workers' retreats were concerned. He frequently requested Fr Devane to be allowed to serve the men at meals. When he received a favourable answer, he donned an apron and acted as server, though his efforts hardly helped from the practical point of view.[107]

In connection with retreats for working men and poor boys, Fr Sullivan came into contact with Frank Duff, founder of the Legion of Mary, an association of Catholic laity who serve the church on a voluntary basis and strive to live and spread the values of the Christian gospel. It was destined to become the largest apostolic organisation of lay people in the Catholic Church, with over 3 million active members. Mr Duff gave this impression of Father Sullivan during his years at Rathfarnham:

> Father Sullivan was always very kind to me personally. He invariably stopped in the street whenever he saw me, in order to exchange a few words, to assure me of his deep interest in the things which I had in hand and to promise his prayers for them. The chief notes which struck me in Father Sullivan were his extreme prayerfulness, his gentleness and humility. Moreover, he gave the impression of being a very mortified man.
>
> My chief picture of him is in his miserable, threadbare garments on a wintry day. I got the impression that he had nothing on underneath. As he walked along (or sometimes ran), he always seemed to be lost in thought, or I suppose it would be more accurate to say, in prayer. I found him an utterly lovable person. The first time I ever saw him in my life, he was on his knees in the domestic chapel in Rathfarnham Castle. That was typical, for I was assured that such was the way in which he spent much of his time. I also heard from a different quarter that he had the reputation of healing, but I never had any direct knowledge of this.[108]

The reference to the typical posture of 'being on his knees' needs to be adapted to 'or on his knee'. Frequently, on short visits to the church, in the prayer before class, even hearing confession, he knelt on just one knee. He paid the price for this while at Rathfarnham. He had to have treatment for bursitis.[109]

During his rectorship, the scholastic Joseph O'Connor, and subsequently Fr Devane, shared a somewhat mysterious experience. Each of them, in turn, occupied a room beneath that of the rector, and were kept awake at night by Fr Sullivan's prayers and by loud sounds as if he was struggling on the floor and being dragged about the room while he cried out 'Oh, oh, oh!' as if in terrible fear. Both men were inclined to think that Fr John was wrestling with some diabolical power. Fr Devane, after a while, could stand it no longer and sought the advice of the spiritual father of the community. The latter volunteered to tell the rector that his prayers were disturbing the rest of another Father. From then on, the sounds ceased entirely.

While in Rathfarnham, Fr John had a greater opportunity of meeting with his brother, William, and his sister, Annie. He had always kept in touch with them. As has been mentioned, he sometimes met with William at his club on St Stephen's Green. William had no difficulty introducing his poorly dressed brother to other club members, and John was unperturbed by his threadbare clothes and his aged and patched boots.

In his years as rector, his gift of calming and consoling those who were suffering mental or physical pain was very much in evidence. At times, moreover, he seemed to be able to see into the minds of those who consulted him, and he spoke of future events with an abrupt and almost disconcerting confidence, which was remarkable in one who was normally reluctant to obtrude his own views. In this, he reminded some people of what they had read of St John Vianey, the Curé d'Ars.[110] As mentioned earlier, so too in this period, some patients, after he spent time in prayer, were told they would be cured, while others were informed that they were soon to go to heaven.

In 1924, Fr Sullivan was replaced as rector of Rathfarnham.

He returned happily to Clongowes. He was 63 years of age, and had only nine more years to live.

CHAPTER SEVENTEEN

Teachings and Maxims

At this point it seems appropriate to view some of his teachings. These were mainly to be found in almost illegible notes scattered across various retreats, or in notes of others who attended his retreats or sought advice from him. They were seldom original. What was convincing was his own emphasis, and his wholeheartedness. A selection of his maxims, teachings, says a great deal about him.

He had this advice for a superior:

1. Be always accessible. Leave Christ in order to find him in your subjects.
2. Always trust those in your care. It is better to err on the side of too much trust.
3. Always be kind.
4. Give praise sometimes. In some convents the faults are always come down on, but there is never a word of praise.
5. Say a prayer to the Holy Ghost every day to ask a right understanding in all things.[111]

Clearly, he tried to live out these requirements in his time as rector. The emphasis on prayer to the Holy Spirit was repeated in many forms.

Prayer and the Holy Spirit

'Without the aid of the Holy Spirit I cannot say "Jesus". The Holy Spirit is the spirit of Jesus.'[112] 'The Holy Ghost is dwelling within us ... Have recourse to the Holy Spirit in all trials, and teach devotion to him. Never undertake any work without asking in prayer for his light.'[113] With regard to difficulties in prayer: 'Keep hammering at the Holy Ghost until he teaches you'.[114]

Observations on Prayer

'When an unexpected humiliation comes to me, I should go to Our Lord in the tabernacle and tell him all about it, and all will be right. I should take all my troubles to the tabernacle. Nothing is too big for Our Lord and nothing is too small'.[115]

'Prayer is the greatest power on earth.'

'Perseverance in prayer is necessary if we want our petitions answered.'

A letter from a poor woman to him said: 'Please pray for me and put your whole heart into it.' There is a great lesson from that woman. So, when you pray, think of her, and put your whole heart into it.

'When we turn to God, God is pleased.' 'He does not need words. Just as an earthly father is satisfied with seeing his child, so is God with us.'

'In prayer, if your thoughts rest on a single word, stay there as long as you can get anything out of it. Imitate a dog with a bone. If you study the dog, you will see that he goes back and back again, gnawing on something that seems to be like a dry useless bone. You wonder what he can get out of it. He has the secret.'[116]

Fr Fergal McGrath, as a novice in 1913, spoke to Fr Sullivan about the difficulty of making an hour's meditation, and received the advice: 'Keep on. Use bits of the Our Father or the Hail Mary. Say anything. But keep on.' (He was disappointed with the advice at the time, but realised later that, as applied to the ways of ordinary prayer, the advice, by its very jejuneness, was sound.)[117]

'In prayer, don't mind the scaffolding, get at God.'

'In temptation, turn your back on it, and throw yourself into prayer.'[118]

Special Prayers

'Have great devotion to the *Rosary*, and teach it to the children. It is the greatest prayer, as it contains the three greatest prayers of the church … It goes straight up to God's throne in heaven.'[119]

'Get the *Magnificat* into your life. Live it, and always be praising and blessing God.'[120]

Fr Fergal McGrath again: as a novice he informed Fr Sullivan that he was feeling depressed. He replied, 'A great cure for depression, there, is to make the *Stations of the Cross*. When you have finished the Stations, you will find all depression gone.' The remarkable thing about the remedy, Fr McGrath observed, was that he had 'never known it to fail'.[121]

At *Mass*, 'Our Lord comes down on the altar, and we can present to him the whole world with its wounds of sin; our country with its festering wounds, and our own souls.'[122]

'*Prayers for our Enemies* are the most powerful of all prayers, and will bring untold blessings on those who utter them.'[123]

For Children

'Teach the children to cling to the heart of Christ, to cling to the cross of Christ, to cling to the Mother of Christ.'

'As artists carve the statues of great men, so should religious try to carve the image of Christ in the souls of children committed to them.'

On Scruples and Uneasiness

'When God forgives me my sins, he buries them beneath a large stone. It is desecration to root them up again.'

'People forget that "I believe in the forgiveness of sins" is an article of faith.'

'Anything that causes uneasiness is from the devil.'[124]

Varia

'To say *Deo Gratias* to all things is to be a saint.'

'God is everywhere, but he does not dwell everywhere, only in faithful souls.'

'Any friend of the poor is a friend of God. That's the nature of the case.'

'Worry won't mend matters.'

God's Mercy

He loved to preach on the Prodigal Son and the Lost Coin. In such a sermon, he observed: 'God always leaves the door un-latched'.

'Worldliness brings a blight on a community and dries up union with God.'[125]

Practical Advice for Life

Words of Fr John Sullivan quoted by the Irish Taoiseach (prime minister), Mr Bertie Ahern, in his final address to Dáil Éireann: 'Take life in instalments, this one day now. At least let this be a good day. Be always beginning. Let the past go. Now let me do whatever I have power to do. (Mr Ahern finished here.) The saints were always beginning. That is how they became saints.' [126]

Finally, some quite distinctive points of emphasis that reflect a strong strand of spirituality from the era of Irish monasticism to Fr Sullivan's own day, and with which, as indicated earlier, many present-day spiritual directors and scripture scholars would not be happy.

Humility

'Try to imitate Jesus. Meekness is all-powerful, few can with-stand it'. Then he adds: 'Do not speak outside confession of your interior life. The devil does much harm that way.'

Self-Denial

'Try to lead a comfortless life. Every victory over self is a victory for God.'

Self-Love

'We shall acquire personal love of Our Lord by going against our own self-love, rooting it out of our hearts. The two cannot exist together. God is jealous of our love. Anything that denies self is an act of love.'[127]

Despite the emphasis in Fr John's life on self-denial and the rooting out of self-love, it would appear that the majority of those who knew him did not find this repellent or oppressive, because it was found in company with lovable qualities such as boundless kindness, transparent sincerity and forgetfulness of self;[128] and where the local people were concerned his austerity was linked to his sanctity and power to heal. One local woman, suffering from cancer, when asked why she came to Fr Sullivan rather than other priests, probably summed up this view: 'He is quite an exception. He is very hard on himself. You have to be hard on yourself to work miracles. And he does it.'[129]

It is interesting to note John Sullivan's affinity to Fr Willie Doyle. Despite their considerable difference in temperament, they shared a deep personal attachment to Christ, often expressed in devotion to the Sacred Heart, and a strong emphasis on penance and self-denial in their lives. After Fr Doyle' death as army chaplain in 1917 and the publication of his life and penances, Fr Sullivan made use of some of Fr Doyle's prayers and quoted his favourite sayings.[130]

CHAPTER EIGHTEEN

The Intensity of the Last Years

A time of change and challenge

On Fr Sullivan's return to Clongowes in 1924, the new Free State government was endeavouring to pull the country together after the ravages of the Civil War, 1921-1923, and faced by internecine strife in the trades union movement. As a strong advocate of the importance of teaching as a profession, he was consciously part of Clongowes long tradition of producing young men to lead and serve in the new Ireland.[131] Prominent among the ministers of government in 1920s were past students, Patrick McGilligan, John Marcus O'Sullivan, Patrick Hogan and Kevin O'Higgins. The last named was a pupil in Clongowes during Father John's first year there. His assassination on 10 July 1927 sent a wave of sadness through the Clongowes community and of shock throughout the country. The spectre loomed of a lapse into anarchy. Prayers for Kevin O'Higgins and his family, and for the country, were offered in the school and among the community.

Two years later the memory of a more famous political figure was celebrated as the centenary of Catholic Emancipation was honoured throughout Ireland. Daniel O'Connell had been a good friend to Clongowes from its inception. He had sometimes stayed there, and he sent his sons to the college. In November that year, the foundation stone was laid of new buildings that were to enable the school to cater more adequately for its school population of 325 boys. Another two years on, the country heaved a sigh of relief at a peaceful transfer of power to a new government, and prepared to welcome a papal nuncio to Dublin, together with Catholic prelates from all over the world, as they came to celebrate a Eucharistic Congress. Once again, Clongowes joined the celebration. That year the nationalist point of view found significant expression in the *Clongownian*'s publication of that year's English Essay that merited the Clongowes Union Gold Medal award. The subject chosen by the college authorities was: '1916 Success or Failure?' The essay examined the cost of the Rising in deaths, imprisonments, the numerous buildings destroyed, and the effect on trade and commerce, but concluded: 'The lethargy of years was cast aside, and a new era of our history dawned. For this we owe all our praise and gratitude to the heroes of 1916. Men who might have lived to be great, died and were greater.'[132]

A multiplicity of healing

Through all these changes and developments, Fr Sullivan found occasions for compassion and thanksgiving and for prayers for all concerned, while he persevered relentlessly in his life of prayer, self-discipline, and response to the needs of others. Once again he became a familiar sight on the roads around Clongowes or further afield. The largest number of his 'cures' occurred in these final years.

On 8 October 1928, a nephew of the late General Michael Collins, also named Michael Collins, was brought to him. The child, aged three years, appears to have been attacked by infantile paralysis, his leg being completely bent up and causing him intense pain. Fr Sullivan promised to say Mass for the child, who was then brought to the Mater Hospital, Dublin, where his condition remained unchanged. On Tuesday, 16 October, his mother, Mrs Sean Collins, who lived in Kildare, received a postcard from Fr Sullivan saying that he had seen Michael and that he was going home well. She hurried to Dublin, and was told by the nun in charge that the child was cured. Fr Sullivan had arrived the preceding evening by bicycle from Clongowes. He prayed for a long time over the child and touched his leg. He then cycled home. Shortly afterwards the nun took the child out of bed, ran a warm bath for him, and to her astonishment he kicked out quite normally with the leg. The trouble never recurred, and the boy grew up strong and well.

Among other well attested 'cures' or healings, the most remarkable occurred in December 1932, only two months before Fr Sullivan's death. It was that of a young married woman who was suffering from pernicious vomiting. She was unable to retain any food and had become practically a living skeleton. She was considered to be in a dying condition and was anointed on 17 December. Her sister brought Fr Sullivan to see her on 22 December. She was only half-conscious and disinclined for any religious consolation. Fr Sullivan sprinkled her with holy water and said some prayers. Next day she seemed slightly better. Next day again, Christmas Eve, she retained food for the first time, and on Christmas Day, to the amazement of her doctor, she was able to eat a Christmas dinner of turkey and ham, and from that she never looked back until she was completely recovered.[133]

There were other instances where a 'cure' did not follow his visit and prayer, but where he seemed to secure for the sick person freedom from physical pain or mental suffering. In 1913, for example, he was asked by a Mr Peter Coonan, a near neighbour to Clongowes, to visit his uncle, Thomas Coonan, who was dying of a bleeding cancer of the throat at his home in Kilclough, near Straffan, Co Kildare. Peter Coonan drove Fr Sullivan in his gig, and when they came near the house they could hear the sick man moaning and crying out in pain. Fr Sullivan prayed over him for a considerable time, and as he rose to go he said, 'Goodbye Tom, and I promise you one thing, that you won't suffer any more.' Thereafter, Tom Coonan had no further pain. He died about a fortnight later. The extraordinary change was commented on by many neighbours.

The ravages of cancer seemed to hold no fear for Fr Sullivan. In 1929, John Nevin, who lived at Betaghstown, near Clongowes, was dying of cancer of the face. One side of his face was almost entirely destroyed. The doctor attending him described it as one of the worst cases he had seen and found it difficult himself to approach the patient. During the last five weeks of the man's life, Fr John visited him every day, and during the last fortnight twice a day. He used to kneel beside the bed for a long time, and the doctor recalled his amazement when he saw him leaning right over the sufferer, with his face almost touching his. A relative added that Fr Sullivan used to put his arms round the poor man in his bed. This kind of fearless compassion evoked from one of the farm workers at Clongowes, on the day of Fr Sullivan's funeral, the concise comment: 'He seemed to take everyone's sorrow and suffering on himself.'[134]

Intimations of a decline

In spite of the severity of his life, Fr Sullivan always enjoyed robust health. In 1929, however, he enquired of the doctor about a friend who had an internal haemorrhage and whether this indicated some internal growth. The doctor put a number of questions and from the readiness of Fr Sullivan's answers he suspected he was talking about himself. In view of the nature of Fr John's final illness, the suspicion was probably correct. Nevertheless, there was no let up in his care for the people of the countryside. In 1931, there were a number of instances of sudden loss of memory, obliging him on one occasion to abandon Mass just before the gospel. He continued working, however, until shortly before his death. In the New Year 1933 he mentioned to one of the nuns in the Presentation Convent in Clane regarding the number of people that were coming to see him, 'They have me killed.' The words were half-jocose, but probably reflected a sense of declining strength.

On 4 February he contacted the doctor about a swelling in the elbow. This was said to be due to bursitis, and the arm was lanced. After this, he was to remain in the college infirmary for about a fortnight. His cheerfulness and patience were remarked on by the nurses. On Thursday 16 February, he wrote probably his last letter. It was in response to a letter from a Mrs Williams, explaining that he had been laid up but assuring her 'the Masses will be said as soon as possible'. He added a postscript emphasising once more his mother's influence: 'P.S. – I owe everything in the world to my dear Mother's tears and prayers and sufferings'.[135]

Final days

The following day he was attacked by a violent internal pain. The doctor, Charles O'Connor of Celbridge, was summoned and judged it was a case for a surgeon. Until the latter could be contacted, the doctor did not give the patient any injection for the intense pain. Fr John remained calm, and to distract his attention from the pain he began to read the breviary. The minister of the house, Fr Patrick Kenny, who looked after the health of the community, tried to remove the breviary but the patient resisted. The minister began to realise that he read the breviary with such a focus of attention that it shut out other matters. He then said to Fr Kenny, 'You had better anoint me, I may die at any moment.' He received the sacrament of Extreme Unction, as it was then known, and made arrangement for the saying of the Masses which he had undertaken. When the surgeon arrived, he diagnosed a dangerous obstruction and ordered the patient to be removed at once to hospital. Two injections were administered, but the pain was so intense that they had little effect. Fr Sullivan suffered greatly whilst travelling in the ambulance to the nursing home of St Vincent's Hospital, at No 96 Lower Leeson Street, Dublin. His ailment, the surgeon, Thomas Lane, later explained, was 'mesenteric thrombosis, causing gangrene of an extensive length of his small intestine. I think it would be very hard for those who have not had a similar type of experience to imagine the appalling intensity of the pain that he had to endure.'

He was operated at 5.00 pm, and in the surgeon's words, 'after his operation he was cheerfulness itself. He was so extraordinarily grateful for what poor service I had been able to give him, and was humorous and confident. His morale was so good that I cheated myself, hoping against hope that he would survive.'[136] The surgeon had been a former student at Clongowes.[137]

Next morning, Fr John was quite conscious and was pleased to greet his brother, Sir William, who had arrived from England by the mail boat. William had succeeded to the baronetcy in 1928 following the death of their brother, Edward. The patient received Holy Communion and spent that day and the following, final day, in almost continuous prayer. His patience was such that it was impossible to know the extent of his suffering. He placed himself entirely in the hands of nurses and doctors. Next day he received Communion once more and continued praying in a strong voice up to midday. At that point the nun in charge, Mother Thecla, thinking that the continuous prayer was excessive in the patient's very weak state, said to him, 'I think you have done enough praying, and you have offered up your sufferings to God, and should now rest.' He agreed, but immediately added, 'But you go on.' The nuns themselves were wearied by these continual prayers, but could not refuse his request. In the afternoon, Fr George Roche, rector of Clongowes, asked for a message for the boys. He whispered, 'God bless and protect them.' About three o'clock he became semi-conscious, and by six he was quite unconscious. Meantime, the countryside around Clongowes was praying and waiting for each fresh bulletin. The post-mistress near the college gate was kept constantly busy answering the anxious queries.

Fr Roche, Sir William Sullivan, Mother Thecla, and a nurse, remained with the patient to the end. During those last hours, William from time to time affectionately kissed his dying brother. As the evening wore on, Sir William began to look exhausted. Mother Thecla suggested that he had done all that was possible, and should now go to his club for the night. He decided that he would wait until 11.00 pm, and if there was no change then he would go. Almost as a final act of consideration, a change was observable about five minutes to eleven. Fr Roche gave a final absolution, and at eleven o'clock John Sullivan died peacefully.

During his closing days, the school was united in prayer for him. After his death the wonder of their situation dawned on the boys. One of them voiced it to a teacher: 'Sir, isn't it a great thing to be able to say you were taught by a saint? And the funny thing is that we knew it, even when we pulled his leg a bit.'[138]

Immediate impact of his death. The funeral

Following his death, as happened so often in the case of men and women distinguished for holiness, the dead man's room was thronged all day with clergy and laity, who came to pray and, if possible, to acquire some 'relic'. Even the young doctors and students of the hospital were noticed taking little locks of his abundant hair.[139] Next day the body was taken to Clongowes, and a Requiem Mass was sung in his 'People's Church', at which Dr Cullen, Bishop of Kildare and Leighlin, presided. Spontaneously at its close, the whole congregation filed up to touch the coffin with rosary beads, crosses or other pious objects. At this demonstration of reverence and affection for his brother, Sir William Sullivan broke down in tears. Then the body was carried down the long straight avenue to the spot where the dead of the college had been placed for over a hundred years. Dr Cullen, Bishop of Kildare and Leighlin, said the prayers at the graveside. When the grave was filled in, and the bishop, priests, and college pupils had gone, many people came to carry to their homes some of the earth from Fr Sullivan's grave.

CHAPTER NINETEEN

Further Developments, Remarkable and Varied

His reputation as a healer led, soon after his death, to people seeking healing through his intercession. A number of them claimed remarkable results and this led, in turn, to Fr McGrath being asked to write a biography of Fr John Sullivan. In preparation for this, much more information was acquired on benefits obtained through his intercession, and the publication of the book, in 1941, brought in hundreds of more testimonies. Further information has continued to arrive over the years. In 1943, the Irish Jesuit provincial, Fr John R. McMahon, sent a questionnaire to a large number of Jesuits who had known Fr Sullivan asking for their opinion as to the desirability of introducing his cause for recognition as a saint. The response was affirmative. In 1944, Fr Sullivan's name was placed on the list drawn up by the postulator of causes in Rome, Fr Carlo Micinelli SJ. The next step was to set up the judicial informative process in the cause of beatification and canonisation. This was required to be conducted in the diocese where the person died. Archbishop John Charles McQuaid, of Dublin, who had known Fr John as a boy, readily gave his approval. The tribunal, consisting of three judges, one of whom was president, one the notary or secretary, and one the promoter of the faith (or 'devil's advocate'), was sworn in at St Francis Xavier's Church, Gardiner Street, in 1947.

The task of the tribunal fell under three headings: the establishment of 'the heroic virtues of the servant of God'; evidence that no undue veneration had been paid to him; and the examination of his writings. The hearing of the evidence was finished in 1953. The work of transcription of the proceedings of the process was completed in 1960. The ten volumes of evidence were signed, sealed, and placed in a specially made oaken chest at Archbishop's House, Dublin, and brought to Rome in the care of Mr Séan Ó hEideáin, Secretary of the Irish Embassy to the Holy See.[140]

The items of evidence included such instances as those given in Fr McGrath's book published in 1941, and a pamphlet, produced much later, entitled *More Memories of Fr John Sullivan*. Here are just two of the briefer accounts of healings after Fr Sullivan's death.

In March 1933, only a month after the death, occurred the case of Mrs G. M. Ryan, of Dublin. She explained:

> I had been ill with heart trouble and pernicious anaemia, and was so bad on March the 19th that I was anointed, the doctor having given up hope of my recovery. I happened to hear of a cure wrought through Rev Father John Sullivan having visited a Mrs. X. It impressed me deeply, and I had a firm belief that if I could get any little relic of his, I should be cured. Thank God, I was favoured with a loan of his sacred stole, and can confidently say that from the moment I received it, I began to regain my strength steadily, invoking his intercession by the following aspiration: 'Rev Father Sullivan, intercede for me through Blessed Virgin Mary and the Sacred Heart of Jesus, if it be God's holy will to cure me.'

Seven years later, in September 1940, the doctor who attended Mrs Ryan made the following statement: 'I saw Mrs. G. M. Ryan last Friday. I remember attending her in 1933 when she was confined to bed with endocarditis and a very advanced form of anaemia. She is now in perfect health, and has a little son about six years of age. In my opinion, her present healthy state is very surprising, and may be accounted for by some supernatural agency.'[141]

The second case was related by a lady who had become friendly with Fr Sullivan when her sons were at school in Clongowes. 'Father Sullivan has interceded for me on many occasions, through Our Lady of Lourdes. It was two weeks after his death, in February 1933, that D – (one of her sons) got a blow in his ear from a snowball. It was such a serious accident that he had to be kept in a darkened room, and the doctor gave it as his opinion that he would never hear again with that ear.'

> I started a novena to Father Sullivan, and asked him to intercede with Our Lady of Lourdes that D – would be cured. At the end of fourteen days, D – surprised the doctor by telling him that he could hear in that ear. The doctor said it was nothing short of a miracle. D – was sent to a Dublin specialist who confirmed what the doctor said, and reported that the hearing of the perforated ear was perfect.

> The doctor consulted in the case, wrote: 'Mr D – X – came under my care in 1933. He had been hit by a snowball over the left side of the head, and sustained a concussion injury of the drumhead of the left ear. There was a perforation of the tymphanic membrane, and pus issued from the middle ear through the aperture for two weeks. He then made a remarkable recovery from the injury, the aperture closed up, and all symptoms disappeared.'[142]

Exhumation

In the furtherance of Fr Sullivan's cause towards beatification, Fr Paolo Molinari SJ, who had been appointed postulator general in 1957, suggested the exhumation of Fr Sullivan's remains and their transfer from Clongowes to St Francis Xavier's Church, Upper Gardiner Street, Dublin. All the required procedures were followed, the remains were placed in a special coffin which stood for the night of 28 September 1960 in the 'People's Church'. The rector of Clongowes celebrated the morning Mass there in the presence of the senior boys and many of the local people. Soon, as the word spread, pilgrims began to arrive. 'All day long, the two avenues to the college were filled with cars and, towards evening, a queue of over a hundred persons was waiting to secure admission to the church. Next morning the flow of pilgrims was renewed, some coming from places far distant. Many invalids were among them. A conservative estimate of those who venerated the remains during the two days was three thousand.'

The coffin was placed in a hearse which left Clongowes at 2.00 pm. On the route as far as Celbridge, Co Kildare, people waited, and many knelt as the hearse passed. Nearing Dublin, the procession was joined by two Garda patrol cars, and a Garda motor cyclist went ahead to warn a special force of Gardaí on duty on the quays and O'Connell Street so that the traffic from the side streets might be stopped. As a result of this organisation – which was quite spontaneously arranged by the Gardaí – the procession reached St Francis Xavier's Church punctually at 4 pm.'[143] It was an imposing tribute to a man who shunned the limelight and sought to be virtually unknown.

The coffin was received on the steps of the church by the Archbishop of Dublin, accompanied by two other bishops, members of the Dublin diocesan chapter, and some 250 Jesuits. The church was crowded although, deliberately, no publicity had been given the proceedings. When the archbishop pronounced the blessing at the high altar, the coffin was brought to the new burial place, adjoining the Sacred Heart chapel. This vault, on the same level as the chapel, was designed by the architect, Andrew Devane, who as a boy in Clongowes had known Fr Sullivan. The design has a simplicity and order in keeping with the man whose remains it shelters.

Thus a remarkable life came to an end. It commenced with a shy, rather earnest boy, with an attractive manner, who was thorough in his studies, and came from a well-to-do and privileged family. As an adult he had a successful career, and had the money and energy to travel throughout Europe and beyond. He could have married well and have enjoyed an opulent, indulgent lifestyle. Instead, he put it all aside. He responded to the story of Christ and his generous self-emptying and began to live a simple life, devoting time and attention to the sick and the poor, and then

felt drawn further – to a vowed life of poverty, chastity and obedience. He endeavoured to live in the presence of the living Christ;
and his whole-hearted nature drew him along a path of resolute
asceticism, an aspect of religious life that has been termed 'the Irish
way', recalling the austerity of the early Irish monks.

The Aftermath

Daily, ever since the remains were laid in the vault, people have
come to pray at the spot, seeking Father John's intercession, as
they did in his lifetime, especially in times of sickness, strain and
sorrow. Many small and larger healings and favours have been
reported. The monthly Mass for his canonisation and in thanksgiving for his life has an attendance of over 200 people from different parts of the country. In the north of Ireland there seems to
be a considerable devotion to John Sullivan: people come in special coaches to visit the shrine, and priests from Gardiner Street
Church have travelled to Newry and other locations in response
to requests for a blessing with Fr Sullivan's cross.

Meantime, the process towards beatification moves slowly in
Rome. The evidence had to be translated into Italian. In 1969, the
Italian version of the evidence was officially accepted by the
Sacred Congregation, and in 1972 the writings of the servant of
God received approval from the Congregation for the Causes of
Saints, an important step on the way.[144]

A Bridge between Traditions

A development that would have cheered John Sullivan has been
the twinning, since 1980, of Clongowes and Portora Royal
School. Beginning with traditional rugby and cricket fixtures, it
has evolved so that every term groups from the two schools visit
each other for a weekend. 'The Portora boys stay in Clongowes,
experiencing the boarding life, while the Clongowes boys stay in
Portora boys' homes. As each group is accompanied by a member of staff, the two staffs also have come to know each other
over the years, and create a continuity which maintains and
deepens the bond.'[145]

A further development that would have brought him, his brother William, and his good friend Judge Murphy, much joy has been the welcome support of the Church of Ireland in various ceremonies honouring his memory. One of John Sullivan's great admirers was the late Church of Ireland archbishop, George Otto Simms. When asked why he was so enthusiastic about Fr John being honoured by the Church of Rome, he responded adroitly 'that we must remember that John was a member of the Church of Ireland into mature adulthood. By then his character would have been well formed. So his holiness he would have learnt in the Anglican tradition and the Roman Catholic Church then reaped the benefits of that solid foundation!'[146]

On 8 May 1983, Dr Simms agreed to give the address at a memorial service to honour John Sullivan's life and work. The service was proposed by members of the Church of Ireland. It took place in St George's Church, Temple Street, Dublin, where John was baptised. Bishop James Kavanagh attended, representing the Catholic archdiocese of Dublin, and brought a special elevation to the occasion by conveying a message of greeting from Pope John Paul II. The text read:

Bishop Kavanagh
Archbishop's House,
Dublin

I am informed that you will participate in the Ecumenical Service of Thanksgiving commemorating the fiftieth anniversary of the death of Fr. John Sullivan.

His Holiness asks you to convey his cordial greetings to all present.

In communion of prayer he gives thanks to Almighty God for the extraordinary gifts bestowed on Fr Sullivan during his life and for the spirit of mutual understanding, reconciliation and good will which his memory enkindles between various Christian communities in Ireland today.

His Holiness prays that this service in St George's Church where Fr Sullivan was first joined to Christ in baptism will bring spiritual joy and comfort to you all.

Cardinal Casareli [147]

In his address, Archbishop Simms provided a well re-searched biographical background to Fr John's life as an Anglican leading to 'when he found his spiritual home in the Jesuit church at Farm Street, London'. Since then there have been other memorial services according to the Anglican rite, and such other eminent figures of the Church of Ireland have preached at these ceremonies as Archbishop Walton Empey, Archbishop Donal Caird, Canon Adrian Empey and Dean Maurice Carey.[148]

Thus, John Sullivan whose life reflected two separate tradi-tions, that of the Protestant ascendancy and that of the majority, less endowed, Catholic population, is proving by his life of prayer and generous service of others a catalyst in bringing closer in 'mutual understanding, reconciliation and good will' leading figures of both traditions; and at a time of renewed political har-mony between the North and South of Ireland, there is an ap-propriateness in hearing words of the son of a Lord Chancellor under British occupation being quoted by the Taoiseach of an Irish Republic as guidelines to follow.

What further does John Sullivan's life signify for readers in the 21st century? Its message will vary from person to person, but, in general, it serves as a call to a manner of life beyond pros-perity and pleasure, beyond consumerism and the need to ac-quire more and more. His simple lifestyle invites one to look be-yond the self as the centre of attention, to be interested in the well-being of others, and to discover, as people have in every century, the spiritual dimension that lifts one's life out of the traffic that tends 'to smother with noise and fog the flowering of the Spirit'.[149] All who met John Sullivan sensed his goodness and felt touched and uplifted by it.

Notes

1. Carton 48, No. 1568, q. Fergal McGrath, *Father John Sullivan, S.J.,* Dublin 1941, p. 8. Virtually everything in the Clongowes Archives is conveyed in Fr McGrath's work, and, as an accessible reference, the work is quoted again and again in the course of this book.
2. Judge M'Bodkin KC, *Recollections of an Irish Judge,* London 1914, p. 135
3. Testimony by Mother Dunne of the Society of the Sacred Heart, a friend of the family, q. McGrath, *op cit,* p. 20
4. McGrath, p. 21
5. Bodkin, *Recollections of an Irish Judge,* p 190
6. Roy Jenkins, *Gladstone,* 1996 ed, pp. 294, 310
7. Q. McGrath, p. 14
8. Letter in Clongowes Wood Archives.
9. McGrath, p. 24
10. Idem
11. Preface to *The Dilemma of John Haughton Steele,* by Joseph Darlington SJ, published 1933
12. McGrath, p. 23
13. Idem, p. 31
14. Idem, p. 32
15. Jenkins, *Gladstone,* p. 361
16. Thomas J. Morrissey, *Towards a National University: William Delany SJ, 1835-1924,* Dublin 1983, p. 214
17. Dr Delany inserted the offending material in his pamphlet *A Plea for Fair Play,* which was circulated to government ministers, politicians, and church men, with the comment that it was not easy 'to imagine a college in Oxford or Cambridge inviting Catholics to become resident students, while allowing one of its leading professors lampoon Catholicism in the college magazine', q. *Towards a National University,* idem.
18. W. B. Stanford & R. B. McDowell, *Mahaffy,* London 1971, Introduction, pp. xi-xii
19. Richard Ellman, *Oscar Wilde,* London 1988, p. 67.
20. Abbot Sir David Hunter Blair, OSB, in *Dublin Review,* July 1938, q. McGrath, p. 45
21. *Freeman's Journal,* 14 April 1885
22. R. Barry O'Brien in *Dublin Castle and the Irish People,* q. McGrath, p. 15
23. T. M. Healy, *Letters and Leaders of My Day,* vol. 1, p. 179
24. Ref. in *Freeman's Journal,* 14 April 1885
25. McGrath, p. 15
26. *Freeman's Journal,* 14 April 1885

27. Idem
28. Mathias Bodkin, *The Port of Tears*, Dublin 1954, p. 19
29. McGrath, pp. 38-9; M. Bodkin, pp. 22-23
30. Bodkin, *Port of Tears*, p. 24
31. Idem, p. 71. Presumably this was while John was at TCD, hence before 1886. His contact with Mary Hayden may have dated from her time teaching at Alexandra College for girls or from her years at the Royal University, 1882-87. See Anna Macdona ed, *From Newman to New Woman*, Dublin 2000, pp. xii-xiii.
32. McGrath, p. 47. 'Finessing' – the skilful handling of a situation. A particular stratagem to gain a point in Whist. 'Cavendish' was the pen name of Henry Jones, a physician, who wrote on Whist. He first compiled a complete system of playing Whist. His book became the authority almost from the date of its appearance in 1862.
33. M. Bodkin, p. 24
34. McGrath, *Father John Sullivan, S.J.*, f.n. p. 42
35. Idem, p. 43
36. Idem, pp. 43-44
37. Idem, pp. 42, 53
38. Idem, pp. 52-3
39. Idem, p. 46
40. Idem, p. 54
41. Idem, pp. 51-2
42. Judge Bodkin, op iam cit, p. 126
43. McGrath, *More Memories of Fr John Sullivan*, p. 4
44. McGrath, *Father John Sullivan, S.J.*, p. 55
45. Idem, p.57
46. Idem, p. 49
47. Quoted in the Google entry for the 'Bridge of Sighs' by Thomas Hood. He is probably best remembered for his poem, 'I remember, I remember, the house where I was born, etc'
48. McGrath, *More Memories ...*, p. 5
49. McGrath, *Fr John Sullivan*, p. 55
50. Idem, pp. 59-61
51. McGrath, *More Memories ...*, pp. 9-10
52. McGrath, *Fr John Sullivan, S.J.*, p. 62
53. M. Bodkin, p. 31
54. McGrath, p. 66
55. Idem, p. 69
56. Idem, pp. 74-5
57. Idem. p. 50
58. Idem, p. 72
59. Idem, p. 66
60. Idem, p. 58
61. Idem, p. 73
62. Idem, p. 75

63. Interviews of Mackey, 30 Nov. 1939; CWC archives.
64. McGrath, *Father John Sullivan, S.J.*, p. 73
65. Idem, pp. 77-78
66. Thomas Hurley, *Michael Browne SJ, 1853-1933*, Dublin 1949.
67. Idem, p. 63
68. Idem, p. 71
69. Idem, p. 73
70. See Albert Nolan OP, *Jesus Today*, Orbis Books NY, 2007, p. 151.
71. McGrath, *Father John Sullivan, S.J.*, pp. 88-90
72. CWC archives.
73. McGrath, op cit, p. 93
74. Idem, p. 91
75. Idem, pp. 96-7
76. The Muratorian Fragment was discovered in the Ambrosian Library, Milan, in 1740. It consisted of some 85 lines and was a copy from the 6th-7th century, but from internal evidence it was clear that the original was of the 2nd century and was the oldest known canon of the New Testament.
77. McGrath, *Father John Sullivan, S.J.*, pp. 100-101
78. Idem, p. 102
79. Idem, p. 106
80. Lieut. General, the Right Hon Sir William Butler, GCR, 1838-1910; educated St Stanislaus College, Tullabeg. Saw service in Africa, Canada, Egypt. Sent on a mission to avert the Boer war, but was highly criticised for his efforts at home; he was knighted, and became well known as lecturer and writer, 1863-1908. His *The Light of the West, 1865-1908*, was to be found in many Irish religious houses, and was first published in 1910.
81. McGrath, pp. 108-11
82. McGrath. *More Memories ...*, pp. 25-29
83. Idem, pp. 30-31
84. McGrath, *Father John Sullivan, S.J.*, p. 112
85. Idem, p. 113
86. McGrath, *More Memories...*, pp. 48-53
87. McGrath, *Father John Sullivan, S.J.*, pp. 198-99
88. Idem, 124-25
89. Idem, 131, 133
90. M. Bodkin, p. 88
91. McGrath, *Father John Sullivan, S.J.*, p. 89
92. Idem, p. 92
93. Idem, p. 94
94. *The Clongowes Union Centenary Chronicle*, Dublin 1997, pp. 98-107
95. Peter Costello, *A History of Clongowes Wood College, 1814-1989*, Dublin 1989, p. 200
96. Idem, p. 202

97. In A. Macdona, ed, *From Newman to New Woman*, Dublin 2001, p. 8
98. McGrath, *More Memories...*, p. 41
99. Idem, pp. 41-42
100. Idem, p. 42
101. McGrath, *Father John Sullivan, S.J.*, p. 259
102. Idem, p. 251
103. McGrath, *More Memories...*, p. 42
104. Idem, p. 45
105. McGrath, *Father John Sullivan, S.J.*, p.52
106. Idem, p. 264
107. Idem. p. 262
108. Idem, p. 263
109. CWC Archives
110. McGrath, *Father John Sullivan, S.J.*, ch. 15, pp. 206 ff., 211
111. Idem, p. 234
112. Idem, p. 233
113. Idem, p. 235
114. McGrath, *More Memories...*, p. 43
115. McGrath, *Father John Sullivan, S.J.*, p. 229
116. Idem, p. 239
117. Idem, pp.218-19
118. Idem, p. 240
119. Idem, 242
120. Idem, p. 240
121. Idem, p. 219
122. Idem, p. 240
123. Idem, p. 233
124. Idem, p. 244
125. Idem, p. 245
126. Idem, p. 238
127. Idem, p. 244
128. Idem, p. 277
129. cit. McGrath in a pamphlet entitled *Fr John Sullivan, S.J.*, Messenger publications, p. 35
130. In white envelope in CWC Archives
131. Apart from ministers, there were public servants such as Joseph Brennan and Joseph Walsh, diplomats D. A. Binchy, Frederick Boland, and Count O'Kelly, and in the Fianna Fáil administration, P. J. Little, Hugo Flinn, and Conor Maguire.
132. *Clongowes Union Centenary Chronicle*, Dublin 1997, p. 108
133. McGrath in pamphlet *Father John Sullivan, S.J.*, pp. 32-33
134. Idem, pp. 34-5
135. McGrath, in the book *Father John Sullivan, S.J.*, pp. 267-9
136. Idem, pp. 269-70
137. Idem, 270; also *More Memories...*, p. 56
138. M. Bodkin, *Port of Tears*, p. 109

139. McGrath, *More Memories...*, pp. 59-60
140. McGrath, in the book *Father John Sullivan, S.J.*, p. 286
141. Idem, pp. 287-9
142. McGrath, *More Memories...*, pp. 63-64
143. Idem, p. 65
144. John Looby SJ, 'Clongowes-Portora Twinning' in *The Clongowes Union Chronicle*, p. 185
145. Conor Harper SJ, 'Father John Sullivan SJ, – A Man for Others' in *The Clongowes Union Centenary Chronicle*, p. 219
146. Idem, p. 220.
147. Idem
148. Idem.
149. From Stephen Spender's poem 'I Think Continually'.

Index